SHILOH NATIONAL MILITARY PARK COMMISSION.

THE BATTLE OF SHILOH

AND THE

ORGANIZATIONS ENGAGED.

COMPILED FROM THE OFFICIAL RECORDS BY
MAJOR D. W REED,
HISTORIAN AND SECRETARY,
UNDER THE AUTHORITY OF THE COMMISSION

1902.

WASHINGTON·
GOVERNMENT PRINTING OFFICE.
1903.

AN ACT To establish a national military park at the battlefield of Shiloh

Be it enacted by the Senate and House of Representatives of the United States of America in Congress assembled, That in order that the armies of the southwest which served in the civil war, like their comrades of the eastern armies at Gettysburg and those of the central west at Chickamauga, may have the history of one of their memorable battles preserved on the ground where they fought, the battlefield of Shiloh, in the State of Tennessee, is hereby declared to be a national military park, whenever title to the same shall have been acquired by the United States and the usual jurisdiction over the lands and roads of the same shall have been granted to the United States by the State of Tennessee, that is to say, the area inclosed by the following lines, or so much thereof as the commissioners of the park may deem necessary, to wit Beginning at low-water mark on the north bank of Snake Creek where it empties into the Tennessee River, thence westwardly in a straight line to the point where the river road to Crumps Landing, Tennessee, crosses Snake Creek, thence along the channel of Snake Creek to Owl Creek, thence along the channel of Owl Creek to the crossing of the road to Purdy, Tennessee, thence southwardly in a straight line to the intersection of an east and west line drawn from the point where the road to Hamburg, Tennessee, crosses Lick Creek, near the mouth of the latter, thence eastward along the said east and west line to the point where the Hamburg Road crosses Lick Creek, thence along the channel of Lick Creek to the Tennessee River, thence along low-water mark of the Tennessee River to the point of beginning, containing three thousand acres, more or less, and the area thus inclosed shall be known as the Shiloh National Military Park *Provided,* That the boundaries of the land authorized to be acquired may be changed by the said commissioners

Sec 2 That the establishment of the Shiloh National Military Park shall be carried forward under the control and direction of the Secretary of War, who, upon the passage of this Act, shall proceed to acquire title to the same either under the Act approved August first, eighteen hundred and eighty-eight, entitled "An Act to authorize the condemnation of land for sites of public buildings, and for other purposes," or under the Act approved February twenty-seventh, eighteen hundred and sixty-seven, entitled "An Act to establish and protect national cemeteries," as he may select, and as title is procured to any portion of the lands and roads within the legal boundaries of the park he may proceed with the establishment of the park upon such portions as may thus be acquired

Sec 3 That the Secretary of War is hereby authorized to enter into agreements whereby he may lease, upon such terms as he may prescribe, with such present owners or tenants of the lands as may desire to remain upon it, to occupy and cultivate their present holdings upon condition that they will preserve the present buildings and roads and the present outlines of field and forest, and that they only will cut trees or underbrush under such regulations as the Secretary may prescribe, and that they will assist in caring for and protecting all tablets, monuments, or such other artificial works as may from time to time be erected by proper authority

Sec. 4 That the affairs of the Shiloh National Military Park shall, subject to the supervision and direction of the Secretary of War, be in charge of three commissioners, to be appointed by the Secretary of War, each of whom shall have served at the time of the battle in one of the armies engaged therein, one of whom shall have served in the Army of the Tennessee, commanded by General U S Grant, who shall be chairman of the commission; one in the Army of the Ohio, commanded by General D C Buell, and one in the Army of the Mississippi, commanded by General A. S Johnston The said commissioners shall have an office in the War Department building, and while on actual duty shall be paid such compensation out of the appropriations provided by this Act as the Secretary of War shall deem reasonable and just, and for the purpose of assisting them in their duties and in ascertaining the lines of battle of all troops engaged and the history of their movements in the battle, the Secretary of War shall have authority to employ, at such compensation as he may deem reasonable, to be paid out of the appropriations made by this Act, some

3

person recognized as well informed concerning the history of the several armies engaged at Shiloh, and who shall also act as secretary of the commission

SEC 5 That it shall be the duty of the commission named in the preceding section, under the direction of the Secretary of War, to open or repair such roads as may be necessary to the purposes of the park, and to ascertain and mark with historical tablets or otherwise, as the Secretary of War may determine, all lines of battle of the troops engaged in the battle of Shiloh and other historical points of interest pertaining to the battle within the park or its vicinity, and the said commission in establishing this military park shall also have authority, under the direction of the Secretary of War, to employ such labor and services and to obtain such supplies and material as may be necessary to the establishment of the said park under such regulations as he may consider best for the interest of the Government, and the Secretary of War shall make and enforce all needed regulations for the care of the park

SEC 6 That it shall be lawful for any State that had troops engaged in the battle of Shiloh to enter upon the lands of the Shiloh National Military Park for the purpose of ascertaining and marking the lines of battle of its troops engaged therein *Provided*, That before any such lines are permanently designated the position of the lines and the proposed methods of marking them by monuments, tablets, or otherwise shall be submitted to and approved by the Secretary of War, and all such lines, designs and inscriptions for the same shall first receive the written approval of the Secretary, which approval shall be based upon formal written reports, which must be made to him in each case by the commissioners of the park *Provided*, That no discrimination shall be made against any State as to the manner of designating lines, but any grant made to any State by the Secretary of War may be used by any other State

SEC 7 That if any person shall, except by permission of the Secretary of War, destroy, mutilate, deface, injure, or remove any monument, column, statues, memorial structures, or work of art that shall be erected or placed upon the grounds of the park by lawful authority, or shall destroy or remove any fence, railing, inclosure, or other work for the protection or ornament of said park, or any portion thereof, or shall destroy, cut, hack, bark, break down, or otherwise injure any tree bush, or shrubbery that may be growing upon said park, or shall cut down or fell or remove any timber, battle relic, tree or trees growing or being upon said park, or hunt within the limits of the park, or shall remove or destroy any breastworks, earthworks, walls, or other defenses or shelter on any part thereof constructed by the armies formerly engaged in the battles on the lands or approaches to the park, any person so offending and found guilty thereof, before any justice of the peace of the county in which the offense may be committed or any court of competent jurisdiction shall for each and every such offense forfeit and pay a fine, in the discretion of the justice, according to the aggravation of the offense, of not less than five nor more than fifty dollars, one-half for the use of the park and the other half to the informer, to be enforced and recovered before such justice in like manner as debts of like nature are now by law recoverable in the several counties where the offense may be committed

SEC 8 That to enable the Secretary of War to begin to carry out the purpose of this Act, including the condemnation or purchase of the necessary land, marking the boundaries of the park, opening or repairing necessary roads, restoring the field to its condition at the time of the battle maps and surveys, and the pay and expenses of the commissioners and their assistant, the sum of seventy-five thousand dollars, or such portion thereof as may be necessary, is hereby appropriated, out of any moneys in the Treasury not otherwise appropriated, and disbursements under this Act shall require the approval of the Secretary of War, and he shall make annual report of the same to Congress

Approved, December 27, 1894

TO SHILOH SOLDIERS.

The Shiloh National Military Park was established by act of Congress in order that, "The armies of the southwest may have the history of one of their memorable battles preserved on the ground where they fought"

It is the desire of the commission having this work in charge that this history shall be complete, impartial, and correct, so that when the monuments of granite and bronze shall have been erected their inscriptions shall publish to the world nothing but the truth

To secure this accuracy all reports have been carefully studied and compared The records at Washington have been thoroughly searched and many who participated in the battle have been interviewed Unfortunately many organizations that served at Shiloh failed to make official reports, others made such meager statements of service that it is difficult to give credit that is doubtless due to gallant organizations. It is, therefore, desired that the statements herein made be earnestly studied by every survivor of Shiloh, particularly in regard to his own organization, and that he report any errors or omissions found in these statements to "Secretary, Shiloh National Military Park Commission, Pittsburg Landing, Tennessee," who will investigate the same and make such corrections as the commission may direct with a view of the publication of a revised edition of this report It is suggested that survivors examine official and other reports carefully and consult surviving comrades so as to be *sure* they are right before asking corrections

CORNELIUS CADLE,
Chairman, Shiloh National Military Park Commission

5

ORGANIZATION OF THE COMMISSION.

Under the provisions of the act of Congress approved December 27, 1894, the Secretary of War appointed as commissioners: Col. Cornelius Cadle, of Cincinnati, Ohio, for Army of the Tennessee, chairman; Gen. Don Carlos Buell, of Paradise, Ky., for Army of the Ohio; Col. Robert F. Looney, of Memphis, Tenn , for Army of the Mississippi; Maj D. W Reed, of Chicago, Ill., secretary and historian, and Capt. James W. Irwin, of Savannah, Tenn , agent for the purchase of land

The commission met and organized April 2, 1895, at Pittsburg Landing, Tenn., and at once entered upon the discharge of its duties, under the direction of the Secretary of War Mr James M. Riddell was appointed clerk of the commission.

Mr Atwell Thompson, civil engineer, of Chattanooga, Tenn., was employed to take charge of the work. Under his direction surveys were made and parallel lines run across the field, from north to south, every 200 feet, upon which stakes were set 200 feet apart. From this survey levels were taken and a contoured topographical map made of all the land within the limits of the park.

Gen. Don Carlos Buell died on November 19, 1898, and Maj. J. H. Ashcraft, late of the Twenty-sixth Kentucky Volunteers was appointed in his place

Col. Robert F. Looney died on November 19, 1899, and Col. Josiah Patterson, late of the First Alabama Cavalry, was appointed in his place.

From official maps and reports, information received from residents, personal recollections of survivors of the battle and other information, roads, fields, and camps were restored, battle lines and positions of troops located and shown on the map and marked by historical tablets on the ground. Four maps have been made which show the field of operations, the approaches to Shiloh, and a map of each day's battle. Copies of these maps accompany this report

The progress of the work has been fully reported each year by the chairman of the commission and his reports published in the annual report of the Secretary of War.

6

SHILOH CAMPAIGN AND BATTLE.

FIELD OF OPERATIONS.[a]

On the 1st day of January, 1862, Gen. Albert Sidney Johnston was in command of all the Confederate forces of Tennessee and Kentucky. His troops occupied a line of defense extending from Columbus, Ky., through Forts Henry and Donelson to Bowling Green, Ky., where General Johnston had his headquarters.

Gen. H. W. Halleck at that date commanded the Department of the Missouri with headquarters at St Louis, and Gen. D. C. Buell commanded the Department of the Ohio with headquarters at Louisville, Ky. The Cumberland River formed the boundary separating the Departments of the Missouri and the Ohio

Various plans had been canvassed by Generals Halleck and Buell, participated in by the general in chief, for an attack upon the Confederate line General Halleck had asked to have General Buell's army transferred to him, or at least placed under his command, claiming that without such union and an army of at least 60,000 men under one commander, it would be impossible to break the well-established lines of General Johnston [b]

Before such union could be effected, and before General Halleck had received a reply to his request, General Grant asked for and received permission to attack the line at Fort Henry on the Tennessee River [c] Assisted by the gunboat fleet of Commodore Foote, Grant captured Fort Henry on the 6th of February, and then moving upon Fort Donelson captured that place with 15,000 prisoners on the 16th The loss of these forts broke General Johnston's line at its center and compelled him to evacuate Columbus and Bowling Green, abandon Tennessee and Kentucky to the Union Army and seek a new line of defense on the Memphis and Charleston Railroad.

General Halleck was displeased with Grant because he sent a division of troops into Buell's department at Clarksville [d] This displeasure was increased when he learned that General Grant had gone to Nashville for consultation with General Buell Halleck directed the withdrawal of Smith's division from Clarksville, suspended General Grant from command, and ordered him to Fort Henry to await orders.[e] He then placed Gen. C. F. Smith in command of all the troops with orders

---

[a] See map of field of operations
[b] No 8 War Records, pp 508–510 Reference to War Records will be given by serial numbers, 10 War Records being volume 10, 11 War Records being part 2 of volume 10
[c] 1 Grant, p 287
[d] Halleck's telegram to Cullum, March 1, 1862.
[e] 11 War Records, p 3

to proceed up the Tennessee River and to make an effort to break the Confederate line on the Memphis and Charleston Railroad at some place near Florence.[a]

General Smith's advance reached Savannah, Tenn., March 13, 1862. Having determined to make that point his base of operations, he landed the troops that accompanied his advance, and sent boats back for supplies and the remainder of his army

Gen W. T. Sherman had organized a division of new troops while he was in command at Paducah. With these he was ordered to report to General Smith. He reached Savannah on the 14th of March and was ordered by General Smith to proceed up the river to some point near Eastport and from there make an attempt to break the Memphis and Charleston Railroad in the vicinity of Burnsville, Miss.[b]

Previous to this time a gunboat fleet had passed up the Tennessee River as far as Florence. At Pittsburg Landing this fleet encountered a small force of Confederates consisting of the Eighteenth Louisiana Infantry, Gibson's battery of artillery, and some cavalry. The gunboats shelled the position and drove away the Confederates. A bursting shell set fire to and destroyed one of the three buildings at the landing The fleet proceeded up the river to Florence and on its return landed a small party at Pittsburg Landing to investigate. This party found a dismounted 32-pounder gun on the river bluff, and about 1 mile out, a hospital containing several Confederate soldiers that had been wounded a few days before in the engagement with the fleet. Near the hospital a Confederate picket post stopped their advance and the party returned to the boats.

In the report made by the officer in command of this naval expedition is found the first mention of Pittsburg Landing, that little hamlet on the Tennessee River so soon to become historic.

When General Sherman's command was passing Pittsburg Landing, Lieutenant Gwin of the U. S. gunboat *Tyler* pointed out to General Sherman the position that had been occupied by the Confederate battery, and informed him that there was a good road from that point to Corinth. That it was, in fact, the landing place for all goods shipped by river to and from Corinth. General Sherman at once reported these facts to General Smith and asked that the place be occupied in force while the demonstration was being made against Burnsville. In compliance with this request, General Hurlbut's division was at once dispatched by boats to Pittsburg Landing.

General Sherman proceeded up the river and landed his division at the mouth of Yellow Creek, a few miles below Eastport, and made an attempt to march to Burnsville. Heavy rains and high water compelled his return to the boats. Finding no other accessible landing place he dropped down to Pittsburg Landing, where he found Hurlbut's division on boats

Sherman reported to General Smith that Eastport was occupied in force by the Confederates, and that Pittsburg Landing was the first point below Eastport that was above water, so that a landing of troops could be made. He was directed to disembark his division and Hurlbut's and put them in camp far enough back to afford room for the other divisions of the army to encamp near the river.

[a] 7 War Records, p 674, 11 War Records, p 6
[b] 10 War Records, p 22

On the 16th of March Sherman landed a part of his division, and accompanied by Colonel McPherson, of General Halleck's staff, marched out as far as Monterey, 11 miles, dispersing a Confederate cavalry camp   Returning to the river he spent two days in disembarking his troops and selecting camps, and on the 19th moved out and put his troops into the positions to which he had assigned them, about 2½ miles from the landing.

Pittsburg Landing, on the left bank of the Tennessee River, 8 miles above Savannah, was at that time simply a landing place for steamboats trading along the river   Its high bluff, at least 80 feet above the water at its highest flood, afforded a safe place for the deposits of products unloaded from, or to be loaded upon, the boats.   From this landing a good ridge road ran southwesterly to Corinth, Miss , 22 miles away.   One mile out from the river the Corinth road crossed another road running north and south parallel with the river, and connecting Savannah below with Hamburg, 4 miles above Pittsburg Landing.   One quarter of a mile beyond this crossing the Corinth road forked, the part known as Eastern Corinth road running nearly south until it intersected the Bark road, 3 miles from the river.

The other, or main road, running due west from the fork, crossed the Hamburg and Purdy road 2 miles from the river, and then turning southwest, passed Shiloh Church just 2½ miles from the river   At a point 5 miles out this main road intersected the Bark road at the southwest corner of what is now the lands of the Shiloh National Military Park.   The Bark road, running nearly due east to Hamburg, forms the southern boundary of the park

On the south side of the Bark road ridge is Lick Creek, which has its rise near Monterey, and empties into the Tennessee about 2 miles above Pittsburg Landing.   North of the main Corinth road, and at an average of about 1 mile from it, is Owl Creek, which flows northeasterly and empties into Snake Creek at the point where the Savannah road crosses it.   Snake Creek empties into the Tennessee River about 1 mile below Pittsburg Landing.

All these streams flow through flat, muddy bottom lands and are, in the spring of the year, practically impassable, and in April, 1862, could not be crossed except at two or three places where bridges were maintained.   These streams therefore formed an excellent protection against an attack upon either flank of an army encamped between them.   The general surface of the land along the Corinth road is about on the same level, but is cut up on either side by deep ravines an water courses leading into the creeks   In many of these ravines are running streams with the usual marshy margins.

In 1862 this plateau was covered with open forest with frequent thick undergrowth and an occasional clearing of a few acres surrounding the farmhouse of the owner.

Sherman selected grounds for his division camps just behind a stream called Shiloh Branch, McDowell's brigade on the right, with his right on Owl Creek at the bridge where the Hamburg and Purdy road crosses the creek.   Buckland's brigade next in line to the left, with his left at Shiloh Church.   Hildebrand's brigade to the left of the church.   Stuart's brigade, detached from others, to the extreme left of the line at the point where the Savannah and Hamburg and the Purdy and Hamburg roads unite just before they cross Lick Creek.

Hurlbut's division formed its camp 1 mile in rear of Sherman's, near the crossing of the Corinth and the Hamburg and Savannah roads.

On the 11th day of March the Departments of the Missouri and the Ohio were consolidated under the name of the Department of the Mississippi, and Maj. Gen H. W. Halleck was assigned to the command, giving him from that date the control he had sought—of both armies then operating in Tennessee. General Smith, about the time of his arrival at Savannah, had received an injury to his leg while stepping from a gunboat into a yawl. This injury, apparently insignificant at first, soon took such serious form that the General was obliged to relinquish command of the troops, and General Grant was restored to duty and ordered by General Halleck to repair to Savannah and take command of the troops in that vicinity Upon his arrival at Savannah, March 17, General Grant found his army divided, a part on either side of the Tennessee River. He at once reported to General Halleck[a] the exact situation, and in answer was directed to "destroy the railroad connections at Corinth "[b]

To carry out this order General Grant transferred the remainder of his army, except a small garrison for Savannah, to the west side of the river, concentrating the First, Second, Fourth, and Fifth divisions at Pittsburg Landing, and the Third at Crump's Landing, 6 miles below. General McClernand with the First Division formed his camp in rear of Sherman's light brigades Gen. W. H L Wallace, commanding the Second Division, encamped to the right of Hurlbut, between Corinth road and Snake Creek. A new division, the Sixth, just organizing under General Prentiss out of new troops, went into camp as the regiments arrived between Hildebrand's and Stuart's brigades of Sherman's division, its center on the eastern Corinth road. Gen. Lew Wallace, commanding the Third Division, placed his first brigade at Crump's, his second brigade at Stony Lonesome, and his third brigade at Adamsville, 5 miles out on the Purdy road.

On March 10 General Halleck wrote General McClellan: "I propose going to the Tennessee *in a few days* to take personal command."[c] Pending his arrival at the front his orders to Smith, to Sherman, and to Grant were: "My instructions not to bring on an engagement must be strictly obeyed,"[d] but when informed by General Grant that the contemplated attack upon Corinth would make a general engagement inevitable, Halleck at once ordered, "By all means keep your forces together until you connect with General Buell Don't let the enemy draw you into an engagement now."[e] To this General Grant replied: "All troops have been concentrated near Pittsburg Landing. No movement of troops will be made except to advance Sherman to Pea Ridge."[f] Sherman made a reconnoissance toward Pea Ridge March 24 and drove some cavalry across Lick Creek He bivouacked at Chambers's plantation that night, and returned to camp next morning

On the 31st, with two regiments of infantry, a section of artillery, and a company of cavalry, Sherman went up to Eastport Finding the Confederate works there and at Chickasaw abandoned, he sent his

[a]11 War Records, p 45
[b]11 War Records, p 46.
[c]11 War Records, p 24
[d]7 War Records, p 674, 10 War Records, p 25, 11 War Records, p. 41
[e]11 War Records, pp 50, 51
[f]11 War Records, p 57.

scouts toward Iuka. Confederate cavalry was encountered, and the command returned to Pittsburg Landing.

The Army of the Tennessee, commanded by Maj. Gen U S Grant, was, on the 5th of April, 1862, composed of six divisions. The First, commanded by Maj. Gen. John A McClernand; the Second, by Brig Gen. W. H. L. Wallace; the Third, by Maj. Gen. Lew. Wallace, the Fourth, by Brig. Gen. S A. Hurlbut; the Fifth, by Biig Gen. W. T. Sherman, and the Sixth, by Brig Gen B. M. Prentiss. Generals McClernand, C F. Smith, and Lew Wallace had been piomoted major-generals March 21, 1862. Official notice of such promotion was sent to General Grant by General Halleck from St. Louis April 5.[a] Previous to this notice of promotion the order of rank of the brigadiers was as follows. Sherman, McClernand, Hurlbut, Prentiss, C. F. Smith, Lew Wallace, W. H L. Wallace General Smith, until relieved by General Grant, March 17, was in command by order of General McClellan.[b]

The camps of Sherman and Prentiss formed the front line about 2½ miles from Pittsburg Landing and extended in a semicircle from Owl Creek on the right to Lick Creek on the left. One company from each regiment was advanced as a picket 1 mile in front of regimental camps.

By the official returns of April 5, 1862, there were, in the five divisions of the Army of the Tennessee at Pittsburg Landing, present for duty,[c] infantry, artillery, and cavalry, officers and men, 39,830; in the Third Division, at Crump's Landing, present for duty, officers and men, 7,564.

On the evening of the 5th the advance of General Buell's army arrived at Savannah, and in one day more would have united with the Army of the Tennessee, ready for the advance on Corinth, as contemplated and announced in General Halleck's programme.

When General Johnston withdrew his army from Kentucky and Tennessee, after the fall of Fort Donelson, he established his new line of operations along the Memphis and Charleston Railroad with his right at Chattanooga and his left on the Mississippi at Fort Pillow. On this line he was reenforced by Generals Polk and Beauregard from Columbus and West Tennessee, and by General Bragg from Pensacola and Mobile, and had ordered Van Dorn, from Little Rock, Ark., to report with his army at Corinth, Miss. As early as March 9, General Ruggles was placed in command at Corinth and was ordered to put his troops in marching order and to commence a line of intrenchments around the town.

On the 29th of March General Johnston issued a general order consolidating the armies of Kentucky and Mississippi, and some independent commands, into the "Army of the Mississippi" of which he assumed the command, naming Gen G. T. Beauregard as second in command and Maj. Gen Braxton Bragg as chief of staff. Subsequently he organized his army into four corps. The First Corps commanded by Maj. Gen. Leonidas Polk; the Second Corps commanded by Maj. Gen. Braxton Bragg; the Third Corps commanded by Maj. Gen. W. J. Hardee, and the Reserve Corps commanded by Brig. Gen. J. C. Breckinridge.

---

[a] 11 War Records, p 94   [b] 11 War Records, p 82   [c] Note

One division of the First Corps, Cheatham's, was at Bethel and Purdy; a brigade of the Second Corps was at Monterey; the Reserve Corps at Burnsville; the cavalry nearer the Union lines. All other troops concentrated at Corinth.[a]

General Johnston had been depressed by the censure of the Southern press, and as late as March 18 offered to relinquish the command of the army to General Beauregard. Reassured by expressions of confidence by Mr. Davis, he resolved to retain command and, if possible, to regain the confidence of the people by taking the offensive and attacking Grant's army at Pittsburg Landing, hoping to defeat that army before it could be reenforced by General Buell.

Hearing that General Buell was nearing Savannah, General Johnston determined to attack at once, without waiting the arrival of Van Dorn. Accordingly, on the 3d of April he issued orders for the forward movement, directing his army to move by the several roads and concentrate at Mickey's, 8 miles from Pittsburg Landing, so as to be ready to attack at sunrise on the morning of the 5th. Heavy rains, bad roads, and the delays incident to marching large columns with wagon trains and artillery over muddy roads, prevented the assembly of the army at Mickey's until nearly night of the 5th. It was then determined to delay the attack until daylight next morning.

The aggregate present for duty, officers and men of the Confederate Army, infantry, artillery, and cavalry, assembled at Mickey's April 5, 1862, as shown by official reports, was 43,968.[b]

This army General Johnston put in line of battle and bivouacked Saturday night in the following order: Major General Hardee's corps on the first or advanced line, with Cleburne's brigade on the left, its left flank at Widow Howell's, near Winningham Creek. Wood's brigade next to the right, with his right on the main Pittsburg and Corinth road, and just in rear of the Wood's field. Shaver's brigade on right of Pittsburg and Corinth road, extending the line nearly to Bark road. As Hardee's line thus deployed did not occupy all the space to Lick Creek, as desired, Gladden's brigade from Withers's division of Second Corps was added to Hardee's right, extending the line across Bark road.

Major General Bragg's corps was deployed 800 yards in rear of the first line, with Ruggles's division on the left and Withers's division on the right, in the following order of brigades from left to right: Pond, Anderson, Gibson, Jackson, and Chalmers. This second line overlapped the first and extended beyond Hardee's on both flanks, Jackson's left flank resting on the Bark road.

The corps of Generals Polk and Breckinridge were formed in column by brigades in rear of the second line. Wharton's and Brewer's cavalry were on the left flank, guarding the roads toward Stantonville. Clanton's cavalry was on the right front, Avery's, Forrest's and Adams's cavalry at Greer's Ford on Lick Creek. Other cavalry organizations were attached to the different corps.

General Johnston's headquarters were established at the forks of the Bark and Pittsburg roads.

Pickets were sent out from the first line. The Third Mississippi, commanded by Major Hardcastle, was on such duty in front of Wood's brigade, his reserve post, at the corner where Wood's and Fraley's fields join.

---

[a] See map of Territory between Pittsburg Landing and Corinth   [b] Note r

13

THE BATTLE.[a]

During the Confederate advance from Monterey on the 3d there had been skirmishing between the cavalry of the two armies, and on the 4th one, of Buckland's picket posts was captured. Buckland sent out two companies in pursuit of the captors These companies were attacked and surrounded by Confederate cavalry, but were rescued by Buckland coming to their relief with his whole regiment On Saturday Generals Prentiss and Sherman each sent out reconnoitering parties to the front. Neither of these parties developed the enemy in force, but reported such evidences of cavalry, that pickets of both divisions were doubled, and General Prentiss, being still apprehensive of attack, sent out at 3 o'clock Sunday morning three companies of the Twenty-fifth Missouri, under Major Powell of that regiment, to again reconnoiter well to the front

Major Powell marched to the right and front, passing between the Rhea and Seay fields, and at 4 55 a m struck Hardcastle's pickets and received their fire The fire was returned by Powell and a sharp engagement was had between these outposts, continuing, as Hardcastle says, one hour and a half, until 6.30 a. m , when he saw his brigade formed in his rear and fell back to his place in line.

Wood's brigade, advancing, drove Powell back to the Seay field, where he was reinforced by four companies of the Sixteenth Wisconsin, that had been on picket near by, and by five companies of the Twenty-first Missouri under Colonel Moore, who at once took command and sent back to camp for the remainder of his regiment

This force, fighting and retreating slowly, was reenforced at southeast corner of the Rhea field by all of Peabody's brigade. Peabody succeeded in holding the Confederates in check until about 8 o'clock, when he fell back to the line of his camp, closely followed by Shaver's brigade and the right of Wood's brigade.

While Peabody's brigade was thus engaged, General Prentiss had advanced Miller's brigade to the south side of Spain field, and placed Hickenlooper's battery to the left and Munch's battery to the right of the Eastern Corinth road. In this position he was attacked by Gladden's brigade and by the left of Chalmers's brigade, that had advanced to the front line. These Confederate brigades, after a stubborn fight, in which Gladden was mortally wounded, drove Miller back to his line of camps at the same time that Peabody was driven back to his. In their several camps Prentiss formed his regiments again and was vigorously attacked by Gladden's and Shaver's brigades, assisted on their left by a part of Wood's brigade, and on the right by Chalmers.

At 9 o'clock Prentiss was driven from his second position with the loss of the entire division camp, two guns of Hickenlooper's battery, and many killed and wounded left on the field Among the killed was Colonel Peabody, the commander of the First Brigade of Prentiss's division.

While the right of Hardee's line was engaged with Prentiss his left had attacked the brigades of Hildebrand and Buckland, of Sherman's division These brigades had formed in line in front of their camps and behind Shiloh Branch, with Barrett's battery at Shiloh Church and Waterhouse's battery to the left, behind the camp of the Fifty-

---

a See maps of first and second days

third Ohio. The Third Brigade of McClernand's division was brought up and formed in support of Sherman's left flank and of Waterhouse's battery. In the Confederate advance the left of Wood's brigade had been slightly engaged with the Fifty-third Ohio, which easily gave way, when Wood obliqued to the right, to avoid Waterhouse's battery, and, following Prentiss, passed the left flank of Hildebrand's brigade, then left wheeled to the attack of McClernand's Third Brigade. Cleburne's brigade, in attempting to cross the marshy ground of Shiloh Branch, received the concentrated fire of the Third and Fourth brigades of Sherman's division, and after two or three unsuccessful efforts to dislodge them, in which his regiments lost very heavily—the Sixth Mississippi having over 70 per cent killed and wounded—he was obliged to give place to Anderson's brigade of Bragg's corps, which was in like manner repulsed with severe loss. Johnson's and Russell's brigades of Polk's corps now came up together. Russell on the right, overlapping Sherman's left, and Johnson to the left across the Corinth road. The reoganized parts of the brigades of Cleburne and Anderson joining Russell and Johnson, the four brigades, assisted by Wood's brigade, advanced, and at 10 o'clock drove Sherman's two brigades, and the Third Brigade of McClernand's division back across the Purdy road with the loss of three guns of Waterhouse's battery and of the camps of the three brigades. During the contest Confederate Generals Clark, commanding a division, and Johnson, commanding a brigade, were severely wounded, and Colonel Raith, commanding McClernand's Third Brigade, was mortally wounded. The capture of the three guns of Waterhouse's battery is claimed by the Thirteenth Tennessee of Russell's brigade, and General Polk seems to concede the claim, though it appears that several regiments were attacking the battery from the front when the Thirteenth Tennessee moved by the right flank and approaching the battery from its left rear reached it before those from the front. General Vaughan, of the Thirteenth Tennessee, says that when his regiment reached these guns a dead Union officer lay near them, and keeping guard over his body was a pointer dog that refused to allow the Confederates to approach the body.

Pond's brigade of Bragg's corps had engaged McDowell's brigade, in conjunction with Anderson's attack on Buckland, and had succeeded in gaining the bridge at McDowell's right flank but had not become seriously engaged when Sherman ordered McDowell to retire and form junction with his Third and Fourth brigades which were then falling back from Shiloh Church. McDowell therefore abandoned his camp to Pond without a contest

After the capture of Prentiss's camps Chalmers's and Jackson's brigades from Bragg's corps were ordered to the right to attack the extreme left of the Union line Preceded by Clanton's cavalry these brigades moved by the flank down the Bark road until the head of the column was at the swampy grounds of Lick Creek, then forming line of battle and placing Gage's and Girardey's batteries upon the bluff south of Locust Grove Creek they compelled Stuart, who was without artillery, to leave his camp and form his lines to left and rear in the timber. Here he held Chalmers in a fierce fight until about 2 o'clock when he fell back to the landing, abandoning the last of Sherman's camps. Jackson's attack, as he came across the creek, fell upon McArthur's brigade, consisting of the Ninth and Twelfth Illinois, sup-

ported on the left by the Fiftieth Illinois and by Willard's battery in the rear. McArthur, in a stubborn contest in which the Ninth Illinois lost 60 per cent of the men engaged, held his ground until Jackson was reinforced by Bowen's brigade of Breckinridge's corps, when McArthur fell back.

When Sherman and Prentiss discovered that they were being attacked by the Confederates in force they asked reenforcements from the divisions in their rear.

McClernand sent his third brigade to reenforce Sherman's left, and Schwartz's battery to assist Buckland. He then formed his First and Second brigades along the Pittsburg road in front of his headquarters; Marsh's brigade, with Burrows's battery on the right; Hare's brigade to the left behind the Review field; McAllister's battery at the northwest corner of said field, and Dresser's battery at Water Oaks Pond. On this line the Third brigade rallied when it fell back from Sherman's line.

Veatch's brigade of Hurlbut's division was sent to reenforce McClernand and formed behind Burrows's battery Hurlbut marched his other brigades to the Peach Orchard and formed line of battle with Williams's brigade facing south and Lauman's brigade facing west. The batteries, Mann's, Ross's, and Myer's, all in the field behind the infantry

W H. L. Wallace's First Brigade, commanded by Colonel Tuttle, moved out on the Eastern Corinth road and formed on the east side of the Duncan field in an old sunken road. McArthur's brigade was disunited. The Eighty-first Ohio and the Fourteenth Missouri were sent to guard the bridge over Snake Creek; the Thirteenth Missouri to reenforce McDowell's brigade and McArthur, in person with the Ninth and Twelfth Illinois and Willard's battery, went to the support of Stuart and formed on his right rear, and at the left of Hurlbut's division, just east of the Peach Orchard. Of Sweeny's brigade, the Seventh and Fifty-eighth Illinois formed on Tuttle's right connecting it with McClernand's left The Fiftieth Illinois was sent to McArthur. The other regiments were held in reserve until about noon when the Eighth Iowa formed on Tuttle's left to fill a gap between Wallace and Prentiss. The Fifty-seventh Illinois went to the extreme left, and the Fifty-second Illinois reported to McClernand at his sixth position just east of Tilghman Creek Batteries D, H, and K, First Missouri Light Artillery, were placed along the ridge in rear of Tuttle Prentiss rallied his broken division, not over 800 men, on Hurlbut's right connecting it with Wallace's left

In the early morning, General Grant at Savannah heard the firing and directed General Nelson, of the Army of the Ohio, to march his division along the east bank of the Tennessee to the point opposite Pittsburg. Then, leaving a request for General Buell to hurry his troops forward as rapidly as possible, he hastened by boat to join his army. Arriving upon the field at about the time that Prentiss was driven from his camp, he immediately dispatched orders to Gen. Lew. Wallace to bring his division to the battlefield. There has ever since been a dispute as to the terms of this order and the time of its delivery. It is admitted that General Wallace received an order, and that he started his command at about 12 o'clock by a road leading into the Hamburg and Purdy road west of the bridge over Owl Creek on the right of Sherman's camps. This bridge was abandoned by McDowell and held

by the Confederates at 10 o'clock An aide from General Grant over-took Wallace on this road about 3 o'clock and turned him back to the Savannah and Hamburg, or river road, by which he reached the battlefield about 7 o'clock p. m.

In the movements of the Confederate troops in the morning Gibson's brigade of Bragg's corps had followed Shaver's brigade and had halted just inside the line of camps This had separated Gibson from Anderson by the length of a brigade; into this space Bragg directed Stephens's brigade, of Polk's corps, and it entered the line of camps in rear of Wood's brigade Stewart's brigade, also of Polk's corps, was sent to the right and entered the line of camps in rear of Gladden's brigade.

When Prentiss was driven back General Johnston ordered his reserve into action by sending Trabue forward on the Pittsburg Landing road to Shiloh Church, while Bowen and Statham were moved down the Bark road and formed line of battle south of the Peach Orchard to the left rear of Jackson and completing the line to where Gladden's brigade, now commanded by Adams, was resting near Prentiss's headquarters camp

Following the capture of the guns of Waterhouses's battery and the retreat of Sherman and Raith to the Purdy road, Wood's and Shaver's brigades, with Swett's battery, were ordered to left wheel Stewart's brigade was sent by left flank along the rear of Peabody's camp to Wood's left where three of the regiments took their places in line, while the Fourth Tennessee, supported by the Twelfth Tennessee, from Russell's brigade, went into line between Wood's and Shaver's brigades. Stanford's battery took position in the camp of the Fourth Illinois Cavalry. Joining this force on its left were the somewhat disorganized brigades of Cleburne, Anderson, Johnson, and Russell General Polk was personally directing their movements and led them forward, without waiting for perfect organization, in pursuit of Sherman's retreating brigades. This combined force of seven brigades moved to the attack of McClernand and Sherman in their second position along the Pittsburg and Purdy road The right of this attacking force, extending beyond McClernand's left, became engaged with W. H. L. Wallace's troops near Duncan House, while Stephens's brigade of Polk's Corps engaged the left of Tuttle's brigade and Prentiss's division in the Hornets' Nest. At the same time Gladden attacked Lauman on west side, of the Peach Orchard. In these attacks Generals Hindman and Wood were disabled, and the Confederates in front of Wallace, Prentiss, and. Lauman were repulsed.

The attack upon McClernand and Sherman was successful, and drove these commands back to the center of Marsh's brigade camp, where they made a short stand at what McClernand calls his third line, and then retired to the field at the right of that camp, to the fourth line. The third and fourth brigades of Sherman's division retired to the landing, and his first brigade, McDowell's, took position on McClernand's right

In the repulse of McClernand from his second and third line he had lost Burrows's entire battery of six guns, which was taken by Wood's brigade; also one gun of McAllister's battery, taken by the Fourth Tennessee, and two guns of Schwartz's battery and four guns of Dresser's battery; part of these, perhaps all, are claimed by the One hundred and fifty-fourth Tennessee.

Rallying in camp of Hare's brigade, McClernand, with McDowell's

brigade on his right, checked the Confederate advance, and then, by a united countercharge, at 12 o'clock, recovered his second brigade camp and his own headquarters, and captured Cobb's Kentucky battery. McClernand gives the Eleventh Iowa and the Eleventh and Twentieth Illinois the credit for the capture of this battery. In the forward movement the Sixth Iowa and the Forty-sixth Ohio of McDowell's brigade, and Thirteenth Missouri of McArthur's brigade, became engaged with Trabue's Confederate brigade in a fierce battle, of which Trabue says.

The combat here was a severe one I fought the enemy an hour and a quarter, killing and wounding 400 or 500 of the Forty-sixth Ohio Infantry, as well as of another Ohio regiment, a Missouri regiment, and some Iowa troops   *   *   *   I lost here many men and several officers

The number killed, wounded, and missing of the Forty-sixth Ohio at the battle of Shiloh, both days, was 246 But of the three regiments opposed to Trabue there were 510 killed, wounded, and missing, most of them were doubtless lost in this conflict So that Trabue may not have seriously erred in his statement.

At the time that McClernand fell back from his second position, General Stewart took command of Wood's and Shaver's brigades, and with the Fourth Tennessee of his own brigade moved to the right and renewed the attack upon Tuttle and Prentiss. Meeting a severe repulse he withdrew at 12 o'clock, with the Fourth Tennessee, to the assistance of the force in front of McClernand. At the same time Shaver's and Wood's brigades retired for rest and ammunition, and Stephens's brigade moved to the right and joined Breckinridge south of the Peach Orchard

General Bragg then brought up Gibson's brigade, which had been resting near Peabody's camp, and sent it in four separate charges against the position held by Prentiss and Tuttle Gibson's brigade was shattered in their useless charges and retired from the field. While Bragg was directing these several movements, Generals Polk and Hardee had renewed the attack upon McClernand and in a contest lasting two hours had driven him back once more to the camp of his First Brigade where he maintained his position until 2.30 p. m , when he fell back across the valley of Tilghman Creek to his sixth line, abandoning the last of his camps.

About 12 o'clock General Johnston, having gotten his reserve in position south of the Peach Orchard, assumed personal command of the right wing of his army and directed a combined forward movement, intending to break the Union left where Chalmers and Jackson had been engaged since about 10 o'clock, in an unsuccessful fight with Stuart and McArthur Bowen's brigade was sent to support Jackson and was closely followed, en échelon to the left, by Statham's, Stephens's, and Gladden's brigades in an attack upon Hurlbut in the Peach Orchard. Stuart, hard pressed by Chalmers and threatened on the flank by Clanton's cavalry, was, as we have seen, the first to yield, and falling back left McArthur's flank exposed, compelling him and Hurlbut to fall back to the north side of the Peach Orchard As Hurlbut's First Brigade fell back, Lauman's brigade on its right was transferred to the left of the division in support of McArthur. Hurlbut's division as then formed stood at a right angle with the line of Prentiss and Wallace.

At 2 30 p. m., while personally directing the movements of his reserve, General Johnston was struck by a minie ball and almost instantly killed.

The death of the Confederate commander in chief caused a relaxation of effort on that flank until General Bragg, hearing of Johnston's death, turned over the command at the center to General Ruggles and, repairing to the right, assumed command, and again ordered a forward movement

General Ruggles, having noted the ineffectual efforts of Bragg to break the Union center, determined to concentrate artillery upon that point. He therefore assembled ten batteries and a section, sixty-two guns, and placed them in position along the west side of the Duncan field and southeast of the Review field. In support of these batteries he brought up portions of the brigades of Gibson, Shaver, Wood, Anderson, and Stewart with the Thirtieth Tennessee and Crescent regiment of Pond's brigade, and once more attacked the position so stubbornly held by Wallace and Prentiss The concentrated fire of these sixty-two guns drove away the Union batteries, but was not able to rout the infantry from its sheltered position in the old road

William Preston Johnston, in the Life of General Albert Sidney Johnston, gives this graphic description of the fighting at this point:

This portion of the Federal line was occupied by Wallace's division and by the remnants of Prentiss's division Here behind a dense thicket on the crest of a hill was posted a strong force of as hardy troops as ever fought, almost perfectly protected by the conformation of the ground To assail it an open field had to be passed, enfiladed by the fire of its batteries It was nicknamed by the Confederates by that very mild metaphor, "The Hornets' Nest " No figure of speech would be too strong to express the deadly peril of an assault upon this natural fortress whose inaccessible barriers blazed for six hours with sheets of flame and whose infernal gates poured forth a murderous storm of shot and shell and musketry fire which no living thing could quell or even withstand Brigade after brigade was led against it, but valor was of no avail Hindman's brilliant brigades which had swept everything before them from the field were shivered into fragments and paralyzed for the remainder of the day Stewart's regiments made fruitless assaults, but only to retire mangled from the field Bragg now ordered up Gibson's splendid brigade, it made a charge, but like the others recoiled and fell back Bragg sent orders to charge again * * * Four times the position was charged Four times the assault proved unavailing, the brigade was repulsed About half past 3 o'clock the struggle which had been going on for five hours with fitful violence was renewed with the utmost fury Polk's and Bragg's corps, intermingled, were engaged in a death grapple with the sturdy commands of Wallace and Prentiss * * * General Ruggles judiciously collected all the artillery he could find, some eleven batteries, which he massed against the position. The opening of so heavy a fire and the simultaneous advance of the whole Confederate line resulted first in confusion and then in defeat of Wallace and the surrender of Prentiss at about half past 5 o'clock Each Confederate commander of division, brigade, and regiment, as his command pounced upon the prey, believed it entitled to the credit of the capture Breckinridge, Ruggles, Withers, Cheatham, and other divisions which helped to subdue these stubborn fighters each imagined his own the hardest part of the work

Generals Polk and Hardee, with the commingled commands of the Confederate left, had followed McClernand in his retreat across Tilghman Creek and about 4 o'clock Hardee sent Pond with three of his regiments and Wharton's cavalry to attack the Union position upon the east side of this creek. In this attack the Confederates were repulsed with heavy loss, the Eighteenth Louisiana alone losing 42 per cent of those engaged. Pond retired to the west side of the creek and took no further part in the action of Sunday. Trabue and Russell, with some other detachments, renewed the attack, and at 4.30 p. m. succeeded in driving McClernand and Veatch back to the Hamburg road, then wheeled to the right against the exposed flank of W. H. L. Wallace's division. At the same time Bragg had forced back the Union left until McArthur and Hurlbut, seeing that they were in

danger of being cut off from the Landing, withdrew their forces, letting the whole of Bragg's forces upon the rear of Prentiss and Wallace, while Polk and Hardee were attacking them on their right flank and Ruggles was pounding them from the front. Wallace attempted to withdraw by the left flank, but in passing the lines, closing behind him, he was mortally wounded. Colonel Tuttle with two of his regiments succeeded in passing the lines while four of Wallace's regiments with the part of Prentiss's division were completely surrounded, and, after an ineffectual effort to force their way back to the Landing, were compelled to surrender at 5.30 p. m. The number of prisoners captured here and in previous engagements was 2,254 men and officers, about an equal number from each division. General Prentiss and the mortally wounded General Wallace were both taken prisoners, but General Wallace was left on the field and was recovered by his friends next day, and died at Savannah, Tenn., four days later.

During the afternoon, Colonel Webster, chief of artillery, on General Grant's staff, had placed Madison's battery of siege guns in position about a quarter of a mile out from the Landing, and then, as the other batteries came back from the front, placed them in position to the right and left of the siege guns. Hurlbut's division as it came back was formed on the right of these guns; Stuart's brigade on the left; parts of Wallace's division and detached regiments formed in the rear and to the right of Hurlbut, connecting with McClernand's left. McClernand extended the line to Hamburg and Savannah road and along that road to near McArthur's headquarters, where Buckland's brigade of Sherman's division, with three regiments of McArthur's brigade, were holding the right which covered the bridge by which Gen. Lew. Wallace was to arrive on the field.

About 5 o'clock Ammen's brigade of Nelson's division of the Army of the Ohio reached the field, the Thirty-sixth Indiana taking position near the left in support of Stone's battery. Two gunboats, the *Tyler* and *Lexington*, were at the mouth of Dill Branch, just above the Landing.

After the capture of Prentiss an attempt was made to reorganize the Confederate forces for an attack upon the Union line in position near the Landing. Generals Chalmers and Jackson and Colonel Trabue moved their commands to the right down the ridge south of Dill Branch until they came under fire of the Union batteries and gunboats, which silenced Gage's battery, the only one with the command. Trabue sheltered his command on the south side of the ridge, while Chalmers and Jackson moved into the valley of Dill Branch and pressed skirmishers forward to the brow of the hill on the north side of the valley, but their exhausted men, many of them without ammunition, could not be urged to a charge upon the batteries before them. Colonel Deas, commanding a remnant of Gladden's brigade, formed with 224 men in the ravine on Jackson's left, and Anderson formed at the head of the ravine, where he remained ten or fifteen minutes, then he retired beyond range of the floating guns. Colonel Lindsay, First Mississippi Cavalry, charged upon and captured Ross's battery, as it was withdrawing from position near Hurlbut's headquarters, and then with 30 or 40 men crossed the head of Dill Branch and attempted to charge another battery, but finding himself in the presence of an infantry force "managed to get back under the hill without damage." This cavalry and the skirmishers from Chalmers' and Jackson's brigades

were the only Confederate troops that came under musketry fire after the Prentiss and Wallace surrender.

In the meantime General Bragg made an effort to get troops into position on the left of Pittsburg road, but before arrangements were completed night came on and General Beauregard ordered all the troops withdrawn The Confederate troops sought bivouacs on the field, some occupying captured Union camps and some returning to their bivouac of Saturday night General Beauregard remained near Shiloh Church General Polk retired to his Saturday night camp. General Bragg was with Beauregard near the church, occupying General Sherman's headquarters camp. General Hardee and General Withers encamped with Colonel Martin in Peabody's camp. Trabue occupied camps of the Sixth Iowa and Forth-sixth Ohio. Pond's brigade alone of the infantry troops remained in line of battle confronting the Union line.

The Union troops bivouacked on their line of battle, extending from Pittsburg Landing to Snake Creek bridge, where the Third Division arrived after dark, occupying the line from McArthur's headquarters to the lowlands of the creek Thirteen hours the battle had raged over all parts of the field without a moment's cessation The Union Army had been steadily forced back on both flanks. The camps of all but the Second Division had been captured, and position after position surrendered after the most persistent fighting and with great loss of life on both sides Many regiments, and brigades even, of both armies had been shattered and had lost their organization Detachments of soldiers and parts of companies and regiments were scattered over the field, some doubtless seeking in vain for their commands; many caring for dead and wounded comrades, others exhausted with the long conflict and content to seek rest and refreshment at any place that promised relief from the terrors of the battle. The fierceness of the fighting on Sunday is shown by the losses sustained by some of the organizations engaged. The Ninth Illinois lost 366 out of 617 The Sixth Mississippi lost 300 out of 425 Cleburne's brigade lost 1,013 out of 2,700, and the brigade was otherwise depleted until he had but 800 men in line Sunday night He continued in the fight on Monday until he had only 58 men in line, and these he sent to the rear for ammunition.

Gladden's brigade was reduced to 224 The Fifty-fifth Illinois lost 275 out of 657 The Twenty-eighth Illinois lost 245 out of 642. The Sixth Iowa had 52 killed outright The Third Iowa lost 33 per cent of those engaged The Twelfth Iowa lost in killed, wounded, and prisoners 98 per cent of the present for duty Only 10 returned to camp, and they were stretcher bearers. These are but samples; many other regiments lost in about the same proportion The loss of officers was especially heavy; out of 5 Union division commanders 1 was killed, 1 wounded, and 1 captured; out of 15 brigade commanders 9 were on the list of casualties, and out of 61 infantry regimental commanders on the field 33 were killed, wounded, or missing, making a loss on Sunday of 45 out of 81 commanders of divisions, brigades, and regiments. The Confederate Army lost its commander in chief, killed; 2 corps commanders wounded; 3 out of 5 of its division commanders wounded; 4 of its brigade commanders killed or wounded, and 20 out of 78 of its regimental commanders killed or wounded. With such losses, the constant shifting of positions, and the length of time engaged, it is not

a matter to cause surprise that the Confederate Army was reduced, as General Beauregard claims, to less than 20,000 men in line, and that these were so exhausted that they sought their bivouacs with little regard to battle lines, and that both armies lay down in the rain to sleep as best they could with very little thought, by either, of any danger of attack during the night

We find at Shiloh that with three exceptions no breastworks were prepared by either side on Sunday night Of these exceptions a Union battery near the Landing was protected by a few sacks of corn piled up in front of the guns, some Confederate regiment arranged the fallen timber in front of Marsh's brigade camp into a sort of defensive work that served a good purpose the next day, and Lieutenant Nispel, Company E, Second Illinois Light Artillery, dug a trench in front of his guns, making a slight earthwork, which may yet be seen, just at the right of the position occupied by the siege guns He alone of all the officers on the field thought to use the spade, which was so soon to become an important weapon of war.

During Sunday night the remainder of General Nelson's division and General Crittenden's division of the Army of the Ohio arrived upon the field, and early Monday morning the Union forces were put in motion to renew the battle. General Crittenden's right rested on the Corinth road, General Nelson, to his left, extending the line across Hamburg road. About 1,000 men [a] from the Army of the Tennessee, extended the line to the overflowed land of the Tennessee Two brigades of General McCook's arriving on the field about 8 o'clock formed on Crittenden's right, Rousseau's brigade in front line and Kirk's in reserve At McCook's right was Hurlbut, then McClernand, then Sherman, then Lew Wallace, whose right rested on the swamps of Owl Creek. The Army of the Ohio formed with one regiment of each brigade in reserve, and with Boyle's brigade of Crittenden's division as reserve for the whole. The remnant of W. H. L. Wallace's division, under command of Colonel Tuttle, was also in reserve behind General Crittenden

The early and determined advance of the Union Army soon convinced General Beauregard that fresh troops had arrived. He, however, made his disposition as rapidly as possible to meet the advance by sending General Hardee to his right, General Bragg to his left, General Polk to left center, and General Breckinridge to right center with orders to each to put the Confederate troops into line of battle without regard to their original organizations. These officers hurried their staff officers to all parts of the field and soon formed a line. Hardee had Chalmers on the right in Stuart's camps, next to him was Colonel Wheeler in command of Jackson's old brigade, then Col Preston Smith with remnants of B R Johnson's brigade; Colonel Maney with Stephens's brigade. Then came Stewart, Cleburne, Statham, and Martin under Breckinridge Trabue, across the main Corinth road, just west of Duncan's, with Anderson and Gibson to his left under Polk. Then Wood, Russell, and Pond under Bragg, finishing the line to Owl Creek Very few brigades were intact, the different regiments were hurried into line from their bivouacks and placed under the command of the nearest brigade officer, and were then detached and sent from one part of the field to another as they were needed to

---

[a] 10 W R , 295 and 338 (Colonel Grose says 15th Illinois, but must be in error.

reenforce thieatened points, until it is impossible to follow movements or determine just where each regiment was engaged

Monday's battle opened by the advance of Gen. Lew. Wallace's division on the Union right, attacking Pond's biigade in Hare's brigade camp, and was continued on that flank by a left wheel of Wallace, extending his right until he had gained the Confederate left flank. Nelson's division commenced his advance at daylight and soon developed the Confederate line of battle behind the peach orchard He then waited for Crittenden and McCook to get into position, and then commenced the attack upon Hardee, in which he was soon joined by all the troops on the field The fighting seems to have been most stubborn in the center, where Hazen, Crittenden, and McCook were contending with the forces under Polk and Breckinridge upon the same ground where W H L. Wallace and Prentiss fought on Sunday

The 20,000 fresh troops in the Union Army made the contest an unequal one, and though stubbornly contested for a time at about 2 o'clock General Beauregard ordered the withdrawal of his army To secure the withdrawal he placed Colonel Looney, of the Thirty-eighth Tennessee with his regiment, augmented by detachments from other regiments, at Shiloh Church, directed him to change the Union center. In this charge Colonel Looney passed Sherman's headquarters and pressed the Union line back to the Purdy road, at the same time General Beauregard sent batteries across Shiloh Branch and placed them in battery on the high ground beyond. With these arrangements, Beauregard, at 4 o'clock, safely crossed Shiloh Branch with his army and placed his rear guard under Breckinridge in line upon the ground occupied by his army on Saturday night. The Confederate Army retired leisurely to Corinth, while the Union Army returned to the camps that it had occupied before the battle

General Beauregard, in his Century "war-book" article, page 64, in speaking of "The second days fighting at Shiloh," says:

Our widely scattered forces, which it had been impossible to organize in the night after the late hour at which they were drawn out of action, were gathered in hand for the exigency as quickly as possible

Generals Bragg, Hardee, and Breckinridge hurried to their assigned positions—Hardee now to the extreme right, where were Chalmers' and Jackson's brigade of Bragg's corps, General Bragg to the left, where were assembled fragments of his own troops, as also of Clark's division, Polk's corps, with Trabue's brigade, Breckinridge was on the left of Hardee This left a space to be occupied by General Polk, who, during the night, had gone with Cheatham's division back nearly to Hardee's position on the night of April 5 But just at the critical time, to my great pleasure, General Polk came upon the field with that essential division

By 7 o'clock the night before all of Nelson's division had been thrown across the Tennessee, and during the night had been put in position between Grant's discouraged forces and our own * * * After exchanging some shots with Forrest's cavalry, Nelson's division was confronted with a composite force embracing Chalmer's brigade, Moore's Texas regiment, with other parts of Withers's division, also the Crescent regiment of New Orleans and the Twenty-sixth Alabama, supported by well-posted batteries, and so stoutly was Nelson received that his division had to recede somewhat Advancing again, however, about 8 o'clock, now reenforced by Hazen's brigade, it was our turn to retire with the loss of a battery But rallying and taking the offensive, somewhat reenforced, the Confederates were able to recover their lost ground and guns inflicting a sharp loss on Hazen's brigade, that narrowly escaped capture Ammen's brigade was also seriously pressed and must have been turned but for the opportune arrival of Terrill's regular battery of McCook's division

In the meantime Crittenden's division became involved in the battle, but was successfully kept at bay for several hours by the forces under Hardee and Breckinridge, until it was reenforced by two brigades of McCook's division, which had been added to the attacking force on the field after the battle had been joined * * *

By 1 o'clock General Bragg's forces on our left, necessarily weakened by the

withdrawal of a part of his troops to reinforce our right and center, had become so seriously pressed that he had called for aid Some remnants of Louisiana, Alabama, and Tennessee regiments were gathered up and sent to support him as best they might, and I went with them personally General Bragg now taking the offensive, pressed his adversary back This was about 2 o'clock My headquarters were still at Shiloh Church

The odds of fresh troops alone were now too great to justify the prolongation of the conflict So, directing Adjutant-General Jordan to select at once a proper position in our near rear, and there establish a covering force including artillery, I dispatched my staff with orders to the several corps commanders to prepare to retire from the field, first making a show, however, at different points of resuming the offensive These orders were executed, I may say, with no small skill, and the Confederate army began to retire at 2 30 p m without apparently the least perception on the part of the enemy that such a movement was going on

The losses of the two days' battle are summed up as follows:

	Killed	Wounded	Missing	Total
General Grant's five divisions	1,472	6,350	2,826	10,648
Gen Lew Wallace's division	41	251	4	296
Total Army of the Tennessee	1,513	6,601	2,830	10,944
Army of the Ohio	241	1,807	55	2,108
Grand total, Union Army	1,754	8,408	2,885	13,047
Confederate Army	1,728	8,012	959	10,699
Total loss at Shiloh	3,482	16,420	3,844	23,746

This gives a Confederate loss of 24⅓ per cent of those present for duty, and a loss in the five divisions of Grant's army present for duty Sunday of 26¾ per cent

It is impossible to give losses of each day separately except as to general officers and regimental commanders These are reported by name, and it is found that casualties among the officers of these grades are as follows

In the five divisions of Grant's army, loss on Sunday........ 45
In the same divisions, loss on Monday............ 2
In Lew Wallace's division, loss on Monday........ 0
In the Army of the Ohio, loss on Monday 3

Total loss general officers and regimental commanders, Sunday and Monday 50

In Confederate Army, casualties to officers of like grade, on Sunday were........ 30
In Confederate Army, Monday.......... 14

Total loss of general officers and regimental commanders, Confederate Army -- 44

No general pursuit of the Confederates was made The orders of General Halleck forbade pursuit,[a] so the Confederates were allowed to retire to Corinth while the Union Army occupied itself in burying the dead and caring for the wounded until General Halleck arrived, and assuming command, inaugurated the "advance upon Corinth," in which the most conspicuous and leading part was played by the spade.

In answer to an inquiry made by the Secretary of War, General Halleck said [b]

The newspaper accounts that our divisions were surprised are *utterly false* Every division had notice of the enemy's approach hours before the battle commenced

Later, in transmitting a map to the Secretary, he said [b]

The impression, which at one time seemed to have been received by the Department, that our forces were surprised in the morning of the 6th, is entirely erroneous I am satisfied from a patient and careful inquiry and investigation that all our troops were notified of the enemy's approach some time before the battle commenced

[a] 11 War Records, pp 97, 104   [b] 10 War Records, p 99

Organization of the Union Army at the battle of Shiloh, Tenn., April 6–7, 1862.

ARMY OF THE TENNESSEE

Maj Gen U S GRANT, Commanding

FIRST DIVISION

Maj Gen JOHN A McCLERNAND

First Brigade

Col ABRAHAM M HARE,[a] 11th Iowa
Col MARCELLUS M CROCKER, 13th Iowa

8th Illinois
        Capt James M Ashmore [a]
        Capt William H Harvey [b]
        Capt Robert H Sturgess
18th Illinois
        Maj Samuel Eaton [a]
        Capt Daniel H Brush [a]
        Capt William J Dillon [b]
        Capt. Jabez J Anderson
11th Iowa, Lieut Col William Hall [a]
13th Iowa, Col Marcellus M Crocker

Second Brigade

Col C CARROLL MARSH, 20th Illinois

11th Illinois·
        Lieut Col Thomas E G Ransom [a]
        Maj Garrett Nevins [a]
        Capt Lloyd D Waddell
        Maj Garrett Nevins
20th Illinois
        Lieut Col Evan Richards [a]
        Capt Orton Frisbie
45th Illinois, Col John E Smith
48th Illinois
        Col. Isham N Haynie [a]
        Maj Manning Mayfield.

Third Brigade

Col JULIUS RAITH, [c] 43d Illinois
Lieut Col ENOS P WOOD, 17th Illinois
17th Illinois
        Lieut Col Enos P Wood
        Maj Francis M Smith
29th Illinois, Lieut Col. Charles M Ferrell.
43d Illinois, Lieut Col Adolph Engelmann.
49th Illinois, Lieut Col Phineas Pease [a]

Unattached

Dresser's Battery (D), 2d Illinois Light Artillery, Capt. James P. Timony.
McAllister's Battery (D), 1st Illinois Light Artillery, Capt Edward McAllister.[a]
Schwartz's Battery (E), 2d Illinois Light Artillery, Lieut George L Nispel
Burrows' Battery, 14th Ohio Light Artillery, Capt Jerome B Burrows.[a]
1st Battalion, 4th Illinois Cavalry, Lieut Col William McCullough.
Carmichael's Company Illinois Cavalry, Capt Eagleton Carmichael
Stewart's Company Illinois Cavalry, Lieut Ezra King

---

[a] Wounded   [b] Killed   [c] Mortally wounded

SECOND DIVISION

Brig Gen. WILLIAM H L WALLACE *a*
Col JAMES M TUTTLE, 2d Iowa

First Brigade

Col JAMES M TUTTLE

2d Iowa, Lt Col James Baker
7th Iowa, Lt Col James C Parrott
12th Iowa
    Col Joseph J Woods *b*
    Capt Samuel R Edgington *c*
14th Iowa, Col Wm T Shaw *c*

Second Brigade

Brig Gen. JOHN McARTHUR *d*
Col THOMAS MORTON, 81st Ohio,

9th Illinois, Col August Mersy
12th Illinois
    Lieut Col Augustus L Chetlain
    Capt. James R Hugunin
13th Missouri, Col Crafts J Wright
14th Missouri, Col B S Compton
81st Ohio, Col Thomas Morton

Third Brigade

Col. THOMAS W SWEENY, *d* 52d Illinois
Col SILAS D BALDWIN, 57th Illinois

8th Iowa, Col James L Geddes *b*
7th Illinois, Maj Richard Rowett
50th Illinois, Col Moses M. Bane *d*
52d Illinois
    Maj Henry Stark.
    Capt Edwin A Bowen
57th Illinois
    Col Silas D Baldwin
    Capt Gustav A Busse
58th Illinois, Col Wm F Lynch *c*

Artillery

Willard's Battery (A), 1st Illinois Light Artillery, Lieut Peter P Wood
Maj J S Cavender's Battalion Missouri Artillery
    Richardson's Battery (D), 1st Missouri Light Artillery, Capt Henry Richardson
    Welker's Battery (H), 1st Missouri Light Artillery, Capt Frederick Welker
    Stone's Battery (K), 1st Missouri Light Artillery, Capt. George H Stone

Cavalry

Company A, 2d Illinois Cavalry, Capt John R Hotaling
Company B, 2d Illinois Cavalry, Capt Thomas J Larison
Company C, 2d United States Cavalry, ⎫
Company I, 4th United States Cavalry, ⎬ Lieut James Powell

---

a Mortally wounded   *b* Wounded and captured   *c* Captured   *d* Wounded

THIRD DIVISION

Maj Gen LEW WALLACE

First Brigade

Col MORGAN L SMITH, 8th Missouri

11th Indiana, Col. George F McGinnis
24th Indiana, Col Alvin P Hovey
8th Missouri, Lieut Col James Peckham

Second Brigade

Col JOHN M THAYER, 1st Nebraska

23d Indiana, Col William L Sanderson
1st Nebraska, Lieut Col William D McCord
58th Ohio, Col Valentine Bausenwein
68th Ohio, Col Samuel H. Steadman *a*

Third Brigade

Col CHARLES WHITTLESEY, 20th Ohio

20th Ohio, Lieut Col Manning F Force
56th Ohio, Col Peter Kinney *a*
76th Ohio, Col Charles R Woods
78th Ohio, Col. Mortimer D Leggett

Artillery

Thompson's Battery, 9th Indiana Light Artillery, Lieut George R Brown
Buel's Battery (I), 1st Missouri Light Artillery, Lieut Charles H Thurber

Cavalry

3d Battalion, 11th Illinois Cavalry, Maj James F Johnson *a*
3d Battalion, 5th Ohio Cavalry, Maj Charles S Hayes *a*

FOURTH DIVISION

Brig Gen STEPHEN A HURLBUT

First Brigade

Col NELSON G WILLIAMS, *b* 3d Iowa
Col ISAAC C PUGH, 41st Illinois

28th Illinois, Col Amory K Johnson
32d Illinois, Col John Logan *b*
41st Illinois
    Col Isaac C Pugh
    Lieut Col Ansel Tupper *d*
    Maj John Warner
    Capt. John H Nale
3d Iowa
    Maj William M Stone *c*
    Lieut George W. Crosley.

---

a Not engaged at Shiloh, remained at Crumps Landing   *c* Captured
b Wounded   *d* Killed.

Second Brigade

Col JAMES C VEATCH, 25th Indiana

14th Illinois, Col Cyrus Hall
15th Illinois
    Lieut Col Edward F W Ellis [a]
    Capt Louis D Kelley
    Lieut Col William Cam, 14th Illinois
46th Illinois
    Col John A Davis [b]
    Lieut Col John J Jones
25th Indiana
    Lieut Col William H Morgan [b]
    Maj John W Foster.

Third Brigade

Brig Gen JACOB G LAUMAN

31st Indiana
    Col Charles Cruft [b]
    Lieut Col John Osborn
44th Indiana, Col Hugh B Reed
17th Kentucky, Col John H McHenry, jr
25th Kentucky
    Lieut Col. Benjamin H Bristow
    Maj William B Wall [b]
    Capt B T Underwood
    Col. John H McHenry, jr , 17th Kentucky

Artillery

Ross's Battery, 2d Michigan Light Artillery, Lieut Cuthbert W Laing
Mann's Battery (C), 1st Missouri Light Artillery, Lieut Edward Brotzmann
Myers's Battery, 13th Ohio Light Artillery, Capt John B Myers

Cavalry

1st and 2d Battalions 5th Ohio Cavalry, Col William H H Taylor

FIFTH DIVISION

Brig Gen WILLIAM T SHERMAN [b]

First Brigade

Col JOHN A McDOWELL, [c] 6th Iowa.

40th Illinois
    Col Stephen G Hicks [b]
    Lieut Col James W Boothe
6th Iowa
    Capt John Williams [b]
    Capt Madison M Walden
46th Ohio, Col Thomas Worthington

Second Brigade

Col DAVID STUART, [b] 55th Illinois
Lieut Col OSCAR MALMBORG, [d] 55th Illinois
Col T KILBY SMITH, 54th Ohio

55th Illinois, Lieut Col Oscar Malmborg
54th Ohio
    Col T Kilby Smith
    Lieut Col James A. Farden
71st Ohio, Col Rodney Mason

[a] Killed   [b] Wounded   [c] Disabled   [d] Temporarily commanding

Third Brigade

Col JESSE HILDEBRAND, 77th Ohio

53d Ohio
  Col Jesse J Appler
  Lieut. Col Robert A Fulton
57th Ohio, Lieut Col Americus V Rice
77th Ohio
  Lieut Col Wills De Hass
  Maj Benjamin D Fearing

Fourth Brigade

Col RALPH P BUCKLAND, 72d Ohio

48th Ohio
  Col Peter J Sullivan *a*
  Lieut Col Job R Parker
70th Ohio, Col Joseph R Cockerill
72d Ohio
  Lieut Col Herman Canfield *b*
  Col Ralph P Buckland

Artillery

Maj EZRA TAYLOR, Chief of Artillery

Taylor's Battery (B), 1st Illinois Light Artillery, Capt Samuel E Barrett
Waterhouse's Battery (E), 1st Illinois Light Artillery
  Capt Allen C Waterhouse *a*
  Lieut Abial R Abbott *a*
  Lieut John A Fitch
Morton Battery, 6th Indiana Light Artillery, Capt Frederick Behr *b*

Cavalry

2d and 3d Battalions 4th Illinois Cavalry, Col T Lyle Dickey
Thielemann's two companies Illinois Cavalry, Capt Christian Thielemann

SIXTH DIVISION

Brig. Gen BENJAMIN M PRENTISS *c*

First Brigade

Col EVERETT PEABODY, *b* 25th Missouri

12th Michigan, Col Francis Quinn
21st Missouri
  Col David Moore *a*
  Lieut Col H M Woodyard
25th Missouri, Lieut Col Robert T. Van Horn
16th Wisconsin, Col. Benjamin Allen *a*

Second Brigade

Col MADISON MILLER, *c* 18th Missouri

61st Illinois, Col Jacob Fry
18th Missouri, Lieut Col Isaac V Pratt *c*
18th Wisconsin, Col. James S Alban *b*

---

a Wounded   *b* Killed   *c* Captured

Not Brigaded

16th Iowa *a*
    Col Alexander Chambers *b*
    Lieut Col Addison H Sanders
15th Iowa, *a* Col Hugh T Reid *b*
23d Missouri *c*
    Col Jacob T Tindall *d*
    Lieut Col Quin Morton *e*

Artillery

Hickenlooper's Battery, 5th Ohio Light Artillery, Capt Andrew Hickenlooper.
Munch's Battery, 1st Minnesota Light Artillery
    Capt Emil Munch *b*
    Lieut William Pfaender

Cavalry

1st and 2d Battalions, 11th Illinois Cavalry, Col Robert G Ingersoll

Unassigned Troops

15th Michigan, *f* Col John M Oliver
14th Wisconsin, *g* Col David E Wood
Battery H, 1st Illinois Light Artillery, Capt Axel Silfversparre
Battery I, 1st Illinois Light Artillery, Capt Edward Bouton
Battery B, 2d Illinois Artillery, siege guns, Capt Relly Madison
Battery F, 2d Illinois Light Artillery, Capt John W. Powell *b*
8th Battery, Ohio Light Artillery, Capt Louis Markgraf

ARMY OF THE OHIO

Maj Gen DON CARLOS BUELL, Commanding

SECOND DIVISION

Brig Gen ALEXANDER McD McCOOK.

Fourth Brigade

Brig Gen LOVELL H ROUSSEAU

6th Indiana, Col Thomas T Crittenden
5th Kentucky, Col Harvey M Buckley
1st Ohio, Col Benjamin F. Smith
1st Battalion, 15th United States, Capt Peter T Swain,
1st Battalion, 16th United States, Capt Edwin F Townsend, } Maj John H King.
1st Battalion, 19th United States, Maj Stephen D Carpenter,

Fifth Brigade

Col EDWARD N KIRK, *b* 34th Illinois

34th Illinois
    Maj Charles N Levanway *d*
    Capt Hiram W Bristol
29th Indiana, Lieut Col David M Dunn
30th Indiana
    Col Sion S Bass *h*
    Lieut Col Joseph B Dodge
77th Pennsylvania, Col Frederick S Stumbaugh

---

a 15th and 16th Iowa were on right in an independent command
b Wounded
c Arrived on field about 9 o'clock April 6
d Killed
e Captured.
f Temporarily attached Monday to Fourth Brigade, Army of the Ohio
g Temporarily attached Monday to Fourteenth Brigade, Army of the Ohio
h Mortally wounded

Sixth Brigade

Col. WILLIAM H. GIBSON, 49th Ohio.

32d Indiana, Col August Willich
39th Indiana, Col Thomas J Harrison
15th Ohio, Maj William Wallace
49th Ohio, Lieut. Col. Albert M Blackman.

Artillery.

Terrill's Battery (H), 5th United States Artillery, Capt William R Terrill

FOURTH DIVISION

Brig Gen WILLIAM NELSON

Tenth Brigade

Col JACOB AMMEN, 24th Ohio

36th Indiana, Col William Grose
6th Ohio, Lieut Col Nicholas L Anderson
24th Ohio, Lieut Col. Frederick C Jones

Nineteenth Brigade

Col WILLIAM B HAZEN, 41st Ohio

9th Indiana, Col Gideon C Moody
6th Kentucky, Col Walter C Whitaker
41st Ohio, Lieut Col George S Mygatt.

Twenty-second Brigade

Col SANDERS D BRUCE, 20th Kentucky

1st Kentucky, Col David A Enyart
2d Kentucky, Col Thomas D Sedgewick
20th Kentucky, Lieut Col Charles S Hanson

FIFTH DIVISION

Brig. Gen THOMAS L CRITTENDEN

Eleventh Brigade

Brig Gen. JEREMIAH T BOYLE

9th Kentucky, Col Benjamin C Grider
13th Kentucky, Col Edward H Hobson
19th Ohio, Col Samuel Beatty
59th Ohio, Col James P Fyffe

Fourteenth Brigade

Col WILLIAM SOOY SMITH, 13th Ohio

11th Kentucky, Col Pierce B Hawkins
26th Kentucky, Lieut Col Cicero Maxwell
13th Ohio, Lieut. Col. Joseph G. Hawkins

Artillery

Bartlett's Battery (G), 1st Ohio Light Artillery, Capt Joseph Bartlett
Mendenhall's batteries (H and M), 4th United States Artillery, Capt. John Mendenhall

SIXTH DIVISION.[a]

Brig Gen THOMAS J WOOD

Twentieth Brigade

Brig Gen JAMES A GARFIELD

13th Michigan, Col Michael Shoemaker
64th Ohio, Col John Ferguson
65th Ohio, Col Charles G Harker

Twenty-first Brigade

Col GEORGE D WAGNER, 15th Indiana

15th Indiana, Lieut Col. Gustavus A Wood
40th Indiana, Col John W Blake
57th Indiana, Col Cyrus C Hines
24th Kentucky, Col. Lewis B Grigsby

---

*Organization of the Confederate Army at the Battle of Shiloh, Tenn.,
April 6-7, 1862.*

ARMY OF THE MISSISSIPPI

Gen ALBERT SIDNEY JOHNSTON [b]
Gen G T BEAUREGARD

FIRST ARMY CORPS

Maj Gen LEONIDAS POLK

FIRST DIVISION

Brig Gen CHARLES CLARK [c]
Brig Gen ALEXANDER P STEWART

First Brigade

Col ROBERT M RUSSELL, 12th Tennessee

11th Louisiana
    Col Samuel F Marks [c]
    Lieut Col Robert H Barrow
12th Tennessee
    Lieut Col Tyree H Bell
    Maj Robert P Caldwell
13th Tennessee, Col Alfred J Vaughan, jr
22d Tennessee, Col Thomas J Freeman [c]
Tennessee Battery, Capt Smith P Bankhead

---

[a] This division arrived upon the field about 2 o'clock on Monday Wagner's brigade reached the front and became engaged, the 57th Indiana losing 4 men wounded
[b] Killed
[c] Wounded

Second Brigade

Brig Gen ALEXANDER P STEWART

13th Arkansas
Lieut Col A D Grayson [a]
Maj James A McNeely [b]
Col James C Tappan
4th Tennessee
Col Rufus P Neely
Lieut Col Otho F Strahl
5th Tennessee, Lieut Col Calvin D Venable
33d Tennessee, Col. Alexander W Campbell [b]
Mississippi Battery, Capt Thomas J Stanford

SECOND DIVISION

Maj Gen BENJAMIN F CHEATHAM [b]

First Brigade

Brig Gen BUSHROD R JOHNSON [b]
Col PRESTON SMITH, 154th Tennessee [b]

Blythe's Mississippi
Col A K Blythe [a]
Lieut Col David L Herron [a]
Maj James Moore
2d Tennessee, Col J. Knox Walker
15th Tennessee
Lieut Col Robert C Tyler [b]
Maj John F Hearn
154th Tennessee (senior)
Col Preston Smith
Lieut. Col Marcus J Wright [b]
Tennessee Battery, Capt Marshall T Polk [b]

Second Brigade

Col WILLIAM H STEPHENS, 6th Tennessee
Col GEORGE MANEY, 1st Tennessee

7th Kentucky
Col Charles Wickliffe [c]
Lieut Col William D Lannom
1st Tennessee (Battalion)
Col George Maney
Maj Hume R Feild
6th Tennessee, Lieut Col Timothy P Jones
9th Tennessee, Col Henry L Douglass
Mississippi Battery, Capt Melancthon Smith.

Cavalry

1st Mississippi, Col Andrew J Lindsay
Mississippi and Alabama Battalion, Lieut Col. Richard H Brewer.

Unattached

47th Tennessee, Col Munson R Hill [d]

---

[a] Killed   [b] Wounded   [c] Mortally wounded.   [d] Arrived on field April 7.

SECOND ARMY CORPS.

Maj Gen BRAXTON BRAGG

Escort

Company Alabama Cavalry, Capt Robert W Smith

FIRST DIVISION

Brig Gen DANIEL RUGGLES

First Brigade

Col RANDALL L GIBSON, 13th Louisiana

1st Arkansas, Col James F Fagan
4th Louisiana
  Col Henry W Allen *a*
  Lieut Col Samuel E Hunter
13th Louisiana
  Maj Anatole P Avegno *b*
  Capt Stephen O'Leary *a*
  Capt Edgar M Dubroca
19th Louisiana
  Col Benjamin L Hodge
  Lieut Col James M Hollingsworth
Vaiden, or Bain's, Mississippi Battery, Capt S C Bain

Second Brigade

Brig Gen PATTON ANDERSON

1st Florida Battalion
  Maj Thaddeus A McDonell *a*
  Capt W G Poole
  Capt W Capers Bird
17th Louisiana, Lieut Col Charles Jones *a*
20th Louisiana, Col August Reichard
Confederate Guards Response Battalion, Maj Franklin H. Clack
9th Texas, Col Wright A. Stanley
Washington (Louisiana) Artillery, Fifth Company, Capt W. Irving Hodgson

Third Brigade

Col PRESTON POND, jr, 16th Louisiana.

16th Louisiana, Maj Daniel Gober
18th Louisiana
  Col Alfred Mouton *a*
  Lieut. Col Alfred Roman.
Crescent (Louisiana) Regiment, Col. Marshall J Smith
Orleans Guard (Louisiana) Battalion, Maj Leon Querouze *a*
38th Tennessee, Col Robert F Looney
Ketchum's Alabama Battery, Capt William H Ketchum

Cavalry

Alabama Battalion (5 companies—Jenkins, Cox, Robins, Tomlinson, and Smith),
Capt Thomas F Jenkins

---

a Wounded.   *b* Mortally wounded.

SECOND DIVISION

Brig Gen JONES M WITHERS

First Brigade

Brig Gen ADLEY H GLADDEN [a]
Col DANIEL W ADAMS, [b] 1st Louisiana
Col ZACH C DEAS, [b] 22d Alabama

21st Alabama
      Lieut Col Stewart W Cayce
      Maj Frederick Stewart
22d Alabama
      Col Zach C Deas
      Lieut Col John C Marrast.
25th Alabama
      Col John Q Loomis [b]
      Maj George D Johnston
26th Alabama
      Lieut Col John G Coltart [b]
      Lieut Col William D Chadick
1st Louisiana
      Col Daniel W Adams
      Maj Fred H Farrar, jr
Robertson's, Alabama, Battery, Capt Felix H Robertson

Second Brigade

Brig Gen JAMES R CHALMERS

      5th Mississippi, Col Albert E Fant
      7th Mississippi, Lieut Col Hamilton Mayson
      9th Mississippi, Lieut Col William A Rankin [a]
      10th Mississippi, Col Robert A Smith
      52d Tennessee, Col Benjamin J Lea
      Gage's, Alabama, Battery, Capt Charles P Gage

Third Brigade

Brig Gen JOHN K JACKSON

      17th Alabama, Lieut Col Robert C Fariss
      18th Alabama, Col Eli S Shorter
      19th Alabama, Col Joseph Wheeler
      2d Texas
            Col John C Moore
            Lieut Col William P Rogers
            Maj Hal G Runnels
      Girardey's, Georgia, Battery, Capt Isadore P Girardey.

Cavalry

Clanton's Alabama Regiment, Col James H Clanton [b]

---

[a] Mortally wounded   [b] Wounded

THIRD ARMY CORPS

Maj Gen WILLIAM J HARDEE.[a]

First Brigade

Brig Gen THOMAS C HINDMAN [b][c]
Col R G SHAVER, 7th Arkansas [b]

2d Arkansas
    Col Daniel C Govan
    Maj Reuben F Harvey
6th Arkansas, Col Alexander T Hawthorn
7th Arkansas
    Lieut Col. John M Dean [d]
    Maj James T Martin
3d Confederate, Col John S Marmaduke
Warren Light Artillery, or Swett's, Mississippi, Battery, Capt Charles Swett.
Pillow's Flying Artillery, or Miller s, Tennessee, Battery, Capt ——— Miller

Second Brigade

Brig Gen PATRICK R CLEBURNE

15th Arkansas, Lieut Col Archibald K Patton [d]
6th Mississippi
    Col John J Thornton [a]
    Capt W A Harper
2d Tennessee
    Col William B Bate [a]
    Lieut Col David L Goodall
5th (35th) Tennessee, Col Benjamin J Hill
23d Tennessee
    Lieut Col James F Neill [a]
    Maj Robert Cantrell
24th Tennessee, Lieut Col Thomas H Peebles

(Shoup's Battalion)

Trigg's (Austin) Arkansas, Battery, Capt John T Trigg
Calvert's (Helena) Arkansas, Battery, Capt J H Calvert
Hubbard's, Arkansas, Battery, Capt George T Hubbard

Third Brigade

Brig Gen STERLING A M WOOD [b]
Col WILLIAM K PATTERSON, 8th Arkansas, temporarily

16th Alabama, Lieut Col John W Harris
8th Arkansas Col William K Patterson
9th (14th) Arkansas (battalion) Maj John H Kelly
3d Mississippi Battalion, Maj Aaron B Hardcastle
27th Tennessee
    Col Christopher H Williams [d]
    Maj Samuel T Love [d]
44th Tennessee, Col Coleman A McDaniel
55th Tennessee, Col James L McKoin
Harper's (Jefferson Mississippi) Battery
    Capt William L Harper [a]
    Lieut Put Darden
Georgia Dragoons, Capt Isaac W Avery

[a] Wounded   [c] Commanding his own and Third Brigade
[b] Disabled.   [d] Killed.

RESERVE CORPS

Brig Gen JOHN C BRECKINRIDGE

First Brigade

Col ROBERT P TRABUE, 4th Kentucky

(Clifton's) 4th Alabama Battalion, Maj James M Clifton
31st Alabama, Lieut Col Montgomery Gilbreath
 3d Kentucky, Lieut Col Benjamin Anderson *a*
 4th Kentucky, Lieut Col Andrew R Hynes *a*
 5th Kentucky, Col Thomas H Hunt
 6th Kentucky, Col Joseph H Lewis
Crew's Tennessee Battalion, Lieut Col James M Crews
Lyon's (Cobb's) Kentucky Battery, Capt Robert Cobb
Byrne's Mississippi Battery, Capt Edward P Byrne
Morgan's Squadron, Kentucky Cavalry, Capt John H Morgan

Second Brigade.

Brig Gen JOHN S BOWEN *a*
Col JOHN D MARTIN

 9th Arkansas Col Isaac L Dunlop
10th Arkansas, Col Thomas D Merrick
 2d Confederate
    Col John D Martin
    Maj Thomas H. Mangum
 1st Missouri, Col Lucius L Rich
Pettus Flying Artillery, or Hudson's Mississippi Battery, Capt Alfred Hudson
Watson's, Louisiana, Battery, ———
Thompson's Company, Kentucky Cavalry, Capt Phil B Thompson

Third Brigade

Col WINFIELD S STATHAM, 15th Mississippi

15th Mississippi
22d Mississippi
19th Tennessee, Col David H Cummings
20th Tennessee, Col Joel A Battle *b*
28th Tennessee
45th Tennessee, Lieut Col Ephraim F Lytle
Rutledge's, Tennessee, Battery, Capt Arthur M Rutledge
Forrest's Regiment Tennessee Cavalry, Col Nathan B Forrest *a*

Unattached

Wharton's Texas Regiment Cavalry, Col John A Wharton *a*
Wirt Adams's Mississippi Regiment Cavalry, Col Wirt Adams
McClung's, Tennessee, Battery, Capt Hugh L W McClung
Roberts Arkansas Battery

---

      a Wounded   *b* Captured

Commanding and staff officers.

DEPARTMENT OF MISSISSIPPI

Maj Gen H W Halleck, commanding
Brig Gen Geo W Cullum, Chief of Staff
Capt N H McLean, assistant adjutant-general
Capt J. C Kelton, assistant adjutant-general
Capt P M Preston, assistant adjutant-general
Col Richard D Cutts, aid-de-camp
Capt C B Throckmorton, aid-de-camp
Lieut J T Price, aid-de-camp
Lieut D C Wagner, aid-de-camp

Lieut A Backer, aid-de-camp
Brig Gen W Scott Ketchum, Inspector-General
Brig Gen A J Smith, Chief of Cavalry
Col J V D Du Bois, Chief of Artillery
Col George Thom, Chief of Engineers
Lieut Col J B McPherson, assistant chief of engineers
Col J C. McKibbin, Judge-Advocate
Maj Robert Allen, Chief Quartermaster
Maj T J Haines, Chief Commissary of Subsistence
Surg J J B Wright, Medical Director.

ARMY OF THE TENNESSEE.

Maj Gen U S Grant, commanding
Col J D Webster, Chief of Staff
Capt J A Rawlins, assistant adjutant-general
Capt W S Hillyer, aid-de-camp
Capt W R Rowley, aid-de-camp
Capt C B Lagow, aid-de-camp
Lieut Col J B McPherson, Chief of Engineers

Lieut W L B Jenney, assistant chief of engineers
Lieut Wm Kossak, assistant chief of engineers
Capt J P Hawkins, Chief Commissary of Subsistence
Surg Henry S Hewitt, Medical Director
Col G G Pride, volunteer aid

FIRST DIVISION

Maj Gen John A McClernand, commanding
Maj Adolph Schwartz,[a] 2d Illinois Artillery, chief of staff
Maj M Brayman, acting assistant adjutant-general
Capt Warren Stewart,[a] Illinois Cavalry, aid-de-camp

Lieut Henry C Freeman,[a] aid-de-camp
Lieut. Jos E Hitt, 4th Illinois Cavalry, aid-de-camp
Lieut A B Hall, 4th Illinois Cavalry, aid-de-camp
Lieut S R Tresilian, assistant engineer
Lieut Erastus S Jones, ordnance officer

First Brigade

Col Abraham M Hare,[a] 11th Iowa, commanding
Lieut. and Adjt Cornelius Cadle, jr , 11th Iowa, acting assistant adjutant-general

Lieut Samuel Caldwell, 8th Illinois, volunteer aid

Second Brigade

Col C C Marsh, 20th Illinois, commanding
Lieut E P Boas, acting assistant adjutant-general
Adjt J E Thompson,[b] 20th Illinois, aid-de-camp

Capt. G W Kennard, acting assistant quartermaster
Surg Christopher Goodbrake, brigade surgeon

Third Brigade

Col Julius Raith,[b] 43d Illinois, commanding
Lieut Abraham H Ryan, acting assistant adjutant-general

---

[a] Wounded.   [b] Killed.

Brig Gen W H L Wallace,[a] commanding
Capt Wm McMichael,[b] assistant adjutant-general
Capt T J Newham, aid-de-camp

Lieut Cyrus E Dickey, aid-de-camp
Lieut Guyton I Davis, 11th Illinois, aid-de-camp
Lieut I P Rumsey, Taylor's Battery, aid-de-camp

First Brigade

Col James M Tuttle, 2d Iowa, commanding

Lieut. Jas P Sample, 7th Iowa, acting assistant adjutant-general

Second Brigade

Brig Gen John McArthur,[c] commanding
Lieut Geo L Paddock, acting assistant adjutant-general

Lieut. George Mason, 12th Illinois, aid-de-camp

Third Brigade

Col Thos W Sweeny,[c] 52d Illinois, commanding
Lieutenant and Adjutant —— Allen, 52d Illinois, acting assistant adjutant-general

Lieut Wm McCullough, 8th Iowa, aid-de-camp

Maj Gen Lewis Wallace, commanding
Capt Frederick Knefler, assistant adjutant-general
Lieut John W Ross, aid-de-camp

Lieut. Addison W Ware, aid-de-camp
Capt E T Wallace, 11th Indiana, aid-de-camp

First Brigade

Col Morgan L Smith, 8th Missouri, commanding

Lieut D C Coleman, acting assistant adjutant-general

Second Brigade

Col John M Thayer, 1st Nebraska, commanding.
Lieut S A Strickland, acting assistant adjutant-general
Capt. Allen Blacker, aid-de-camp
Lieut. William S. Whittin, aid-de-camp

Lieut Col Robt K Scott, 68th Ohio, volunteer aid
Capt. Lewis Y Richards, 68th Ohio, volunteer aid
Mr. Geo. E. Spencer, volunteer aid

Third Brigade.

Col Charles Whittlesey, 20th Ohio, commanding.

E N Owens, acting assistant adjutant-general

Brig Gen. Stephen A Hurlbut, commanding
Capt Smith D Atkins, acting assistant adjutant-general
Lieut. J C Long, 9th U S Infantry, aid-de-camp
Lieut M. K Cook, aid-de-camp

Capt S Simmons, acting commissary of subsistence
Lieut D J Benner, assistant quartermaster
Surg A G Keenan, medical director
Lieut W H Dorchester, volunteer aid

First Brigade

Col N G. Williams,[c] 3d Iowa, commanding

Lieut F Sessions, acting assistant adjutant-general.

---

[a] Killed [b] Captured. [c] Wounded.

Second Brigade

Col. James C Veatch, 25th Indiana, commanding
Capt F. W Fox, 14th Illinois, acting assistant adjutant-general

Lieutenant —— Brunner, 25th Indiana, aid-de-camp
Surg John T Walker, brigade surgeon.

Third Brigade

Brig Gen Jacob G Lauman, commanding
Lieut. H Scofield, [a] acting assistant adjutant-general

Lieut T N Barnes, aid-de-camp

FIFTH DIVISION

Brig Gen Wm T Sherman,[a] commanding
Capt J H Hammond, assistant adjutant-general
Maj W. D Sanger, volunteer aid
Lieut John Taylor, 5th Ohio, aid-de-camp
Lieut W D Strong, assistant quartermaster

Lieut J C McCoy, 54th Ohio, aid-de-camp
Maj Ezra Taylor, chief of artillery
Capt. C A Morton, 32d Illinois, acting commissary of subsistence
Surg D W Hartshorn, medical director
Asst Surg Saml L'Hommedieu, assistant medical director
Lieut Wm Kossak, engineer

First Brigade

Col J A McDowell, 6th Iowa, commanding
Lieut Byron K Cowles, 6th Iowa, acting assistant adjutant-general (absent)

Capt Willard H Harland, 6th Iowa, aid-de-camp

Second Brigade

Col David Stuart,[a] 55th Illinois, commanding.

Adjt Charles Loomis, aid-de-camp

Third Brigade

Col Jesse Hildebrand, 77th Ohio, commanding

Lieut S S McNaughton, acting assistant adjutant-general

Fourth Brigade

Col. Ralph P Buckland, 72d Ohio, commanding
Lieut Eugene A Rawson, 72d Ohio, acting assistant adjutant-general

John B Rice, surgeon
Lieut D M Harkness, 72d Ohio, quartermaster

SIXTH DIVISION

Brig Gen Benj M Prentiss,[b] commanding
Capt Henry Binmore, assistant adjutant-general

Lieut Edwin Moore, aid-de-camp
Surg S W Everett,[c] division surgeon.

First Brigade

Col Everett Peabody,[c] 25th Missouri, commanding

Capt Geo K Donnelly, assistant adjutant-general

Second Brigade

Col Madison Miller, 18th[b] Missouri, commanding

---

[a] Wounded. [b] Captured [c] Killed

ARMY OF THE OHIO.

Maj Gen Don Carlos Buell, commanding
Col James B Fry, Chief of Staff
Capt J M Wright, assistant adjutant-general
Lieut A F Rockwell, aid-de-camp
Lieut C L Fitzhugh, 4th U S Artillery, aid-de-camp
Lieut T J. Bush, 24th Kentucky, aid-de-camp

Capt J H Gilman, 19th U S , Inspector of Artillery
Capt E Gay, 16th U S , Inspector of Cavalry
Capt H C Bankhead, 5th U S , Inspector of Infantry
Capt Nathaniel Michler, engineer
Surg Robt Murray, U S A , Medical Director.

SECOND DIVISION

Brig Gen Alex McD McCook, commanding
Capt Daniel McCook, assistant adjutant-general
Lieut S W Davies, aid-de-camp
Lieut W T Hoblitzell, aid-de-camp

Lieut W F Straub, aid-de-camp
Capt Orris Blake, provost-marshal
Capt J D Williams, acting commissary of subsistence
Lieut J A Campbell, ordnance officer
Surg A P Meylert, medical director.

Fourth Brigade

Brig Gen Lovell H Rousseau, commanding
Lieut D Armstrong, acting assistant adjutant-general
Lieut David Q Rousseau, aid-de-camp

Lieut John D Wickliffe, 2d Kentucky Cavalry, aid-de-camp
Capt W M Carpenter, assistant quartermaster
Mr E F Jewett, volunteer aid

Fifth Brigade

Col Edward N Kirk,[a] 34th Illinois, commanding
Capt S T Davis, 77th Pennsylvania, acting assistant adjutant-general

Capt Abraham Beehler, 34th Illinois, aid-de-camp
Lieut S B Dexter, 34th Illinois, aid-de-camp

Sixth Brigade

Col W H Gibson, 49th Ohio, commanding
Capt Henry Clay, assistant adjutant-general

Lieut Wm C Turner, aid-de-camp
Lieut E A Otis, aid-de-camp
Surg S W Gross, brigade surgeon

FOURTH DIVISION

Brig Gen William Nelson, commanding
Capt J Mills Kendrick, U S Volunteers, assistant adjutant-general
Lieut Wm P Anderson, 6th Ohio, aid-de-camp
Lieut Richard Southgate, 6th Ohio, aid-de-camp
W Preston Graves, volunteer aid
Horace N Fisher, volunteer aid

Capt J G Chandler, U S Army, assistant quartermaster
Lieut C C Peck, 6th Ohio, acting commissary of subsistence
Lieut Chas C Horton, 24th Ohio, ordnance officer
Capt and Asst Surg B J D Irwin, U S Army, medical director

Tenth Brigade

Col Jacob Ammen, 24th Ohio, commanding

Lieut R F Wheeler, aid-de-camp

Nineteenth Brigade

Col Wm B Hazen, 41st Ohio, commanding
Lieut Robt L Kimberly, acting assistant adjutant-general

Lieut Chas D Gaylord, aid-de-camp
Lieut Wm M Beebe, jr , aid-de-camp.

---

a Wounded

Twenty-second Brigade

Col Sanders D Bruce, 20th Kentucky, commanding
Lieut. S T. Corn, acting assistant adjutant-general

Lieut Wickliffe Cooper, aid-de-camp

FIFTH DIVISION

Brig Gen Thos L Crittenden, commanding
Capt Lyne Starling, assistant adjutant-general

Lieut Louis M Buford, aid-de-camp
Surg Middleton Goldsmith, medical director

Eleventh Brigade

Brig Gen J T Boyle, commanding
Capt John Boyle, assistant adjutant-general
Lieut H Q Hughes, aid-de-camp

Lieut H T Liggett, aid-de-camp
Lieut John T Farris, acting assistant quartermaster

Fourteenth Brigade

Col Wm Sooy Smith, 13th Ohio, commanding
Lieut Frank J Jones, 13th Ohio, acting assistant adjutant-general

Lieut R E Hackett, 26th Kentucky, aid-de-camp

SIXTH DIVISION

Brig Gen Thos J Wood, commanding
Capt Wm H Schlater, assistant adjutant-general
Capt Geo W Lennard, 36th Indiana, aid-de-camp
Capt. Fred A Clark, 29th Indiana, aid-de-camp
Lieut Col Isaac Gass, 64th Ohio, inspector-general

Lieut Clark S Gregg, 65th Ohio, acting commissary of subsistence
Lieut Frank B Hunt, 65th Ohio, ordnance officer
Lieut John C Martin, 21st Ohio, signal officer
Surg Francis B Mussy, medical director

Twentieth Brigade

Brig Gen James A Garfield, commanding

Twenty-first Brigade

Col Geo D Wagner, 15th Indiana, commanding

CONFEDERATE ARMY.

Gen Albert Sidney Johnston,[a] commanding
Maj Gen Braxton Bragg, Chief of Staff
Capt H P Brewster, assistant adjutant-general
Capt N Wickliffe, assistant adjutant-general
Lieut George Baylor, aid-de-camp
Lieut Thomas M Jack, aid-de-camp
Governor Isham G Harris, volunteer aid
Col Wm Preston, volunteer aid

Maj D M Hayden, volunteer aid
Dr E W Munford, volunteer aid
Calhoun Benham, volunteer aid
Capt Theodore O'Hara, assistant inspector-general
Maj Albert J Smith, assistant quartermaster
Capt W L Wickham, assistant quartermaster
Col J F Gilmer,[b] Chief Engineer
Surg D W Yandell, Medical Director

---

[a] Killed   [b] Wounded.

Gen G T BEAUREGARD, second in command, commanding, Monday

Col Thomas Jordan, assistant adjutant-general
Lieut John W Otey, assistant adjutant-general
Lieut Col S W Ferguson, aid-de-camp
Lieut A R Chisolm, aid-de-camp
Brig Gen James Trudeau, volunteer aid
Capt W W Porter, volunteer aid
Maj Geo W Brent, assistant inspector-general

Col R B Lee, Chief of Subsistence.
Capt Clifton H Smith, assistant adjutant-general
Col Jacob Thompson, volunteer aid
Maj Numa Augustine, volunteer aid
Maj H E Peyton, volunteer aid
Capt Albert Ferry, volunteer aid
Capt B B Waddell, volunteer aid
Capt. E H Cummins, Signal Officer

FIRST CORPS

Maj Gen Leonidas Polk, commanding
Maj Geo Williamson,ᵃ assistant adjutant-general
Lieut W B Richmond, aid-de-camp
Lieut A H Polk, aid-de-camp
Lieut P B Spence, aid-de-camp
Lieut John Rawle, aid-de-camp
Lieut John S Lanier, aid-de-camp
Lieut W M Porter, volunteer aid

Lieut Col E D Blake, assistant inspector-general
Maj Smith P Bankhead, Chief of Artillery
Capt J T Champneys, Chief of Ordnance
Maj Thomas Peters, assistant quartermaster
Surg W D Lyles, Medical Director

FIRST DIVISION

Brig Gen Charles Clark,ᵃ commanding
Capt W H McCardle, assistant adjutant-general
Lieut Wm Yerger, jr , aid-de-camp
Maj W H Haynes,ᵃ acting commissary of subsistence
James E McClure, assistant quartermaster

Maj Howell Hinds, assistant adjutant-general, Army of Potomac, volunteer aid
Maj W M Inge, assistant adjutant-general, Army of Potomac, volunteer aid
Capt John A Buckner, 8th Kentucky, volunteer aid

First Brigade.

Col R M Russell, 12th Tennessee, commanding

Second Brigade

Brig Gen A P Stewart, commanding
Capt Thomas W Preston,ᵇ assistant adjutant-general

Lieut N Green, jr , aid-de-camp
Col W B Ross, volunteer aid.
Mr Joseph D Cross, volunteer aid

SECOND DIVISION

Maj Gen B F Cheatham,ᵃ commanding
Maj James D Porter, assistant adjutant-general
Capt F H McNairy, aid-de-camp
Capt T F Henry, aid-de-camp

A L Robertson, aid-de-camp
John Campbell,ᵇ aid-de-camp
Judge Archibald Wright, volunteer aid
Col Edward Pickett, jr , 21st Tennessee, volunteer aid
Capt Wm Roundtree, volunteer aid

First Brigade

Brig Gen B R Johnson,ᵃ commanding
Maj G G Rogers, assistant adjutant general
Capt Wm T Blakemore, aid-de-camp

Capt D. L Moore, volunteer aid
Capt John H Anderson,ᵃ 10th Tennessee, volunteer aid

Second Brigade

Col Wm H Stephens, 6th Tennessee, commanding
Lieut Isaac M Jackson,ᶜ assistant adjutant-general

Wm. D Stephens,ᵃ aid-de-camp.
Thos. A Henderson,ᵃ aid-de-camp.
Capt. A L Swingley, volunteer aid.

ᵃWounded   ᵇ Killed   ᶜMortally wounded

SECOND ARMY CORPS

Maj Gen Braxton Bragg, commanding
Maj George G Garner, assistant adjutant-general
Capt. H. W Walter, assistant adjutant-general
Capt G B Cooke, assistant adjutant-general
Lieut Towson Ellis, aid-de-camp
Lieut F S Parker, aid-de-camp
Lieut Col F Gardner, C S Army, assistant inspector-general
Lieut Col W K Beard,[a] Florida Volunteers, assistant inspector-general.

Capt S H Lockett, chief engineer
Maj J H Hallonquist, Chief of Artillery
Capt W O Williams, assistant chief of artillery
Capt H Oladowski, Chief of Ordnance
Maj J J Walker, Chief of Subsistence
Maj L F Johnston, Chief Quartermaster.
Maj O P Chaffee, assistant quartermaster
Surg A J Foard, Medical Director
Surg J C Nott, Medical Inspector
Lieut. Col David Urquhart, volunteer aid

FIRST DIVISION

Brig Gen Daniel Ruggles, commanding
Capt Roy M Hooe, assistant adjutant-general
Lieut M B Ruggles, aid-de-camp
Maj. E S Ruggles,[a] volunteer aid
Capt G M Beck, volunteer aid
Col S S Heard, 17th Louisiana, volunteer aid

Maj J H Hallonquist, chief of artillery
Maj. John Claiborne, chief quartermaster
Lieut L D Sandidge, assistant inspector-general
Surg F M Hereford,[a] medical director
Dr S S Sandidge, volunteer surgeon

First Brigade

Col Randall L Gibson, 13th Louisiana, commanding
Lieut Benjamin King,[b] aid-de-camp

Lieut H H Bein, acting assistant adjutant-general
Mr Robert Pugh, aid-de-camp

Second Brigade

Brig Gen Patton Anderson, commanding
Capt William G Barth, assistant adjutant-general
Lieut Wm M Davidson, aid-de-camp
Lieut John W James, 5th Georgia, aid-de-camp

Capt. Henry D Bulkley, acting commissary of subsistence
Capt John T. Sibley, assistant quartermaster
Surg C B Gamble, medical director.
Lieut Wm McR Jordan,[a] 1st Florida, aid-de-camp

Third Brigade

Col Preston Pond, jr , commanding

Lieut O O Cobb, assistant adjutant-general

SECOND DIVISION

Brig Gen Jones M Withers, commanding
Capt D E Huger, assistant adjutant-general
Lieut D F Withers, aid-de-camp

Lieut B M Thomas, assistant inspector-general
R W Withers, volunteer aid
S B Howe, volunteer aid
Wm Williamson, volunteer aid
L E Smith, volunteer aid.

First Brigade

Brig Gen A H Gladden,[c] commanding
Maj C. D Anderson, acting assistant adjutant-general
Adjt Adolph Kent, 1st Louisiana, aid-de-camp

Adjt John Stout, 25th Alabama, aid-de-camp
Adjt Elias F Travis, 22d Alabama, aid-de-camp.
Sergt Maj —— Nott, 22d Alabama, aid-de-camp

---

[a] Wounded   [b] Killed.   [c] Mortally wounded.

Second Brigade

Brig Gen James R Chalmers, commanding
Capt Henry Craft, assistant adjutant-general
Lieut Geo T Banks, aid-de-camp

Lieut W T Stricklin, 3d Mississippi, assistant inspector-general.
Capt R S Crump, acting commissary of subsistence.
Lieut M M Shelley, volunteer aid
Mr James Barr, volunteer aid

Third Brigade

Brig Gen John K Jackson, commanding

Capt J B Cummings, assistant adjutant-general

THIRD ARMY CORPS

Maj Gen Wm J Hardee,[a] commanding
Maj W D Pickett, assistant adjutant-general
Lieut John R B Burtwell, aid-de-camp.
Lieut Thomas W Hunt,[a] aid-de-camp
Capt William Clare,[a] aid-de-camp
Lieut ——— Wilson, aid-de-camp
Capt A W Clarkson, aid-de-camp

Maj F A Shoup, Chief of Artillery
Lieut Wm Kearney, assistant inspector-general
Maj L O Bridewell, Chief Quartermaster
Maj W E Moore, Chief Commissary
Surg G W Lawrence, Medical Director
Col S H Perkins, volunteer aid

First Brigade

Col R G Shaver, 7th Arkansas, commanding

Second Brigade

Brig Gen P R Cleburne, commanding

Maj J K Dixon, assistant adjutant and inspector-general

Third Brigade

Brig Gen S A M Wood,[a] commanding
Lieut Linus A McClung, assistant adjutant-general
Lieut H. C Wood, aid-de-camp
Capt Wm Clare,[a] volunteer aid

Capt Joshua Sledge,[a] volunteer aid
Capt J H Coleman, volunteer aid.
Mr Frank Foster, volunteer aid
Lieut S Church, acting commissary of subsistence

RESERVE CORPS

Brig, Gen John C Breckinridge, commanding

First Brigade.

Col Robt P Trabue, 4th Kentucky, commanding
Joseph L Robertson, assistant adjutant-general
Capt Samuel Gray, volunteer aid

John Hooe, volunteer aid
Thomas B. Darragh, volunteer aid
Robt. W McKee, volunteer aid
Charlton Morgan,[a] volunteer aid.
Charles J Maston, volunteer aid

Second Brigade

Brig Gen John S Bowen,[a] commanding

Third Brigade.

Col Winfield S Statham, 15th Mississippi, commanding

---

[a] Wounded

DETAILED MOVEMENTS OF ORGANIZATIONS.

THE ARMY OF THE TENNESSEE

On the 6th day of April, 1862, the Army of the Tennessee was encamped on the west bank of the Tennessee River, the First, Second, Fourth, Fifth, and Sixth Divisions at Pittsburg Landing, with 39,830 officers and men present for duty; the Third Division at Crump's Landing, with 7,564 officers and men present for duty.

General Grant's headquarters was at Savannah, Tenn., where he was awaiting the arrival of General Buell While at breakfast early Sunday morning, April 6, General Grant heard heavy firing at Pittsburg Landing, and leaving orders for General Nelson to move his division up the east bank of the river to Pittsburg, General Grant and staff repaired to the battlefield, where he arrived at about 8 a. m. He visited each of his divisions at the front, and finding that the attack was by a large force of the enemy, he sent an order for his Third Division to hasten to the field and a request to General Buell for reenforcements The Army of the Tennessee was gradually driven back until at sunset it occupied a position extending from the Landing to Snake Creek Bridge. In this position it repulsed an attack made by the Confederates at 6 o'clock p. m.

General Grant passed the night in bivouac with his troops, without shelter, and early next morning, reenforced by his Third Division and by General Buell with three divisions of the Army of the Ohio, he renewed the battle, and at 4 p. m. had regained possession of the entire field.

FIRST DIVISION.

(McClernand's)

This division, composed of three brigades of infantry, four batteries of artillery, one battalion and two companies of cavalry, was ordered from Savannah to Pittsburg March 20, 1862, and went into camp across the main Corinth road about one-half mile east of Shiloh Church. On Sunday morning, April 6, 1862, the division formed for battle with its Third Brigade thrown forward to support Sherman's left; its First and Second Brigades along the Corinth road; McAllister's battery at the northwest corner of the Review field, Burrows's battery at center of second brigade; Dresser's battery at Water Oaks Pond; Schwartz's battery, first to Sherman's right, then at the crossroads. The division was attacked at about 9 a. m and was driven from its position along the Corinth road at about 11 a. m. with the loss of Burrows's battery, one gun of McAllister's battery, and one gun of Schwartz's battery It made its next stand at right angles to the center of its Second-Brigade camp, where Dresser's battery lost four guns. The division then retired to its fourth line, in the camp of its First Brigade, where it rallied and in a countercharge drove the Confederates back and recovered the whole of the camp of the Second Brigade and McClernand's headquarters, and captured Cobb's Kentucky battery at 12 m. It held this advance but a short time, when it was driven slowly back until at 2 p m it was again in the field of its First-Brigade camp, where it held its fifth line until 2 30 p. m. It then retired across Tilghman Creek to its sixth line, at "Cavalry Field," where at 4.30 p. m. it

repulsed a charge made by Pond's brigade and Wharton's cavalry, and then retired to the Hamburg and Savannah road, where, with its left thrown back, it bivouacked Sunday night.

It advanced Monday morning over the same ground where it fought on Sunday, and at 4 p. m. reoccupied its camps on the field.

First Brigade.

(Hare's)

This brigade of four regiments, forming the right of the First Division, was encamped in Jones Field It moved from its camp at about 8 a. m. April 6, 1862, by the left flank and formed in line of battle on the ridge between the Review field and the Corinth road, its left in edge of Duncan Field, in the following order from left to right: Eighth Illinois, Eighteenth Illinois, Thirteenth Iowa. The Eleventh Iowa, detached from the brigade, formed still farther to the right, supporting Dresser's battery at the Water Oaks Pond.

In this position the three left regiments were attacked about 10 a. m. by Shaver's brigade of Hardee's corps, and at 11 a m. were driven back across the Corinth road, the left behind the north side of Duncan Field. This position was held until McClernand advanced and recovered his camp at noon. These regiments then retired with the division, the Thirteenth Iowa participating in the repulse of Wharton's cavalry on sixth line at 4 30. Here Colonel Hare was wounded, and Col. M M. Crocker, Thirteenth Iowa, took command of the brigade and conducted the three regiments to bivouac near the Fourteenth Iowa camp. The Eleventh Iowa, in support of Dresser's battery, fell back to the third and fourth lines with its division, and in the rally and recovery of camps it captured a standard from the enemy, and in conjunction with the Eleventh and Twentieth Illinois captured Cobb's battery. The regiment then fell back and at night was, still supporting the two remaining guns of Dresser's battery, in position at the left of the siege guns.

On Monday this brigade was attached to Tuttle's command, which served as reserve for General Crittenden's division, Army of the Ohio, until about 3 p. m , when it was ordered to the front and charged the enemy southwest of Review field, the Eighth and Eighteenth Illinois each capturing one gun from the enemy.

Second Brigade.

(Marsh's)

This brigade of four regiments was encamped, with its left in Woolf Field, in the following order of regiments from left to right: Forty-fifth Illinois, Forty-eighth Illinois, Twentieth Illinois, Eleventh Illinois. It formed line of battle on its parade ground Sunday morning, April 6, 1862, and at about 8 a m. moved out, first to the front, but immediately afterwards to the left, and formed along the Corinth road, its left at the northwest corner of the Review field, its right near the crossroads, Burrows's battery at the center.

In this position the brigade was fiercely attacked by Wood's brigade of Hardee's corps and Stewart's brigade of Polk's corps. It withstood the attack from about 10 a. m. to 11 a. m , when it fell back about 700 yards and re-formed at right angles to the center of its camp. It held this position for a short time and then fell back to Jones Field, where it rallied and in conjunction with other troops recaptured its

camp at about noon. In this advance the Twentieth and Eleventh Illinois, assisted by the Eleventh Iowa, captured Cobb's Confederate battery. The brigade retained possession of parts of its camp for about two hours, retiring slowly to Jones Field, where it was engaged until 2 30 p. m., when it fell back to Hamburg and Savannah road, where its three left regiments united with the Third Brigade and bivouacked Sunday night, just south of McArthur's headquarters The Eleventh Illinois, reduced to a captain and 80 men, bivouacked near the siege guns, and was in reserve on Monday. The Twentieth, Forty-fifth, and Forty-eighth formed a part of Marsh's command on Monday and advanced nearly west, recovering their camps at about 3 p. m.

Third Brigade

(Raith's)

This brigade of four regiments was camped along the Hamburg and Purdy road, its right near the left of the Second Brigade, in the following order from left to right: Forty-ninth Illinois, Forty-third Illinois, Twenty-ninth Illinois, Seventeenth Illinois.

Colonel Rearden, senior officer present, being sick, Colonel Raith was informed, after his regiment was in line of battle, that he was to command the brigade. Under orders from division commander, he moved the right of his brigade forward to Shiloh Church to the support of Sherman's left. In this position the brigade was attacked about 9 a. m. April 6, 1862, on its left flank by Wood and Stewart and in front by Russell and Johnson, and was driven slowly back to the crossroads, where it joined the right of the Second Brigade. Here the Seventeenth and Forty-third, while supporting Schwartz's battery, were subjected to a crossfire of artillery and lost heavily. Colonel Raith was mortally wounded. The Forty-third was surrounded and cut its way out, losing 43 men killed, that were buried in one trench near the crossroads. Lieutenant Colonel Wood, who succeeded to the command of the brigade, did not hold his brigade intact. The Seventeenth and Forty-third rallied at McClernand's third line and again at his fourth position, where they were joined by the Forty-ninth. The Seventeenth and Forty-ninth then retired to Hamburg and Savannah road. The Forty-third was engaged in the advance and retaking of the camp at noon, and then joined the Seventeenth and Forty-ninth at Hamburg and Savannah road, where the three regiments were engaged at 4 30 p. m., and bivouacked Sunday night. On Monday these regiments joined Marsh's command and served with him until the enemy retired from the field The Twenty-ninth was engaged at Cavalry Field in resisting Pond's attack at 4 30 p. m., after which it retired to siege guns, where it remained Sunday night and Monday. McAllister's battery lost one gun at northwest corner of review field, and was afterwards engaged in McClernand's fifth and sixth positions, and at the landing at 6 p. m., and on Monday, with Marsh's brigade.

SECOND DIVISION.

(W H. L. Wallace's)

This division, composed of three brigades of infantry, four batteries of artillery, and four companies of cavalry, was commanded by Brig. Gen C. F. Smith until April 2, 1862, when, on account of Smith's disability, Brig. Gen. W. H. L. Wallace was assigned to the command.

The division arrived at Pittsburg Landing March 18 and established
its camp near the river between the Corinth road and Snake Creek   It
formed at 8 a. m. Sunday morning, April 6th, when the First and
Second Brigades and three batteries were conducted by Wallace to a
position on Corinth road just east of Duncan Field, where Tuttle's
brigade was formed south of the road, and two regiments of Sweeny's
brigade on north side of the road.   The other regiments of Sweeny's
brigade were held in reserve for a time and then distributed to different parts of the field.   McArthur's brigade was detached from the
division and served on other parts of the field.   Batteries D, H, and
K, First Missouri Light Artillery, were placed on a ridge behind
Tuttle's brigade   In this position Wallace was attacked at about 9.30
a m by Shaver's brigade, assisted by artillery located in the Review
field.   At 10 30 a m. the attack was renewed by Shaver, Stephens,
and Stewart, followed at noon by four determined attacks by Gibson's
brigade.   General Ruggles then took charge of the Confederate forces
in front of Wallace and assembled ten batteries and two sections of
artillery on the west side of Duncan Field, and sent Wood, Anderson,
Stewart, and Cleburne to reenforce Shaver in a renewed attack upon
Wallace's front.   At the same time the Union forces on Wallace's
right and left retired, allowing the enemy to gain his flanks and rear.
Seeing that he was being surrounded, Wallace sent his batteries to the
rear and then attempted to move his infantry out by the flank along
the Pittsburg road.   While riding at the head of his troops and near
the fork of the Eastern Corinth road he received a mortal wound and
was left for dead upon the field.   When that part of the field was
recovered on Monday General Wallace was found to be alive   He
was taken to Savannah, where he died on the 10th.   Four regiments
of the division did not receive orders to retire in time to save them-
selves and were surrounded and captured at 5.30 p. m.   The remainder
of the division, under the command of Colonel Tuttle, retired to the
right of the siege guns where the troops remained in line Sunday
night.

On Monday the infantry commanded by Tuttle acted as reserve to
Crittenden's division of the Army of the Ohio, until about noon, when
it advanced to front line on Crittenden's right and participated in all
the after battles of the day.

Battery A, First Illinois Light Artillery, served with McArthur's
brigade on Sunday and had three guns in action with Sherman on
Monday.   The three Missouri batteries, when they retired from Wallace's line at 5 p. m., reported to Colonel Webster near the Landing
and were put in line, where they assisted in repelling the last Confederate attack on Sunday.   They were not engaged on Monday.

First Brigade

(Tuttle's)

This brigade of four regiments was encamped near the river north of
the Corinth road.   It moved to the front Sunday morning, April 6,
1862, by the Eastern Corinth road.   When near southeast corner of
Duncan field, Colonel Tuttle, riding at the head of his brigade, discovered the enemy in the woods beyond the field.   He at once turned
the head of his brigade to the right and threw his regiments into line
in an old road behind Duncan Field in the following order from left

to right: Fourteenth Iowa, Twelfth Iowa, Seventh Iowa, Second
Iowa The right reaching to the Coiinth road, the left extending
one iegiment beyond, oi south of, Eastern Corinth road, the thiee
right iegiments behind a field; the left regiment behind a dense
thicket. About 9 30 a. m Confederate batteries opened fire upon the
brigade. This was soon followed by infantry attack coming through
the thick brush on the left. At about 10.30 a m. Stephens's brigade
made an attack through the field. He was repulsed when he reached
the middle of the field. This was closely followed by a second attack
by Stephens, assisted by General Stewart, commanding Hindman's
division. About noon Gibson's brigade was sent against Tuttle's
position, and made four determined but unsuccessful charges
lasting until aftei 2 p m., when it withdrew and Shaver made his
third attack, in which Lieutenant Colonel Dean of the Seventh Arkansas was killed within a few yards of the front of the Fouiteenth Iowa.
General Ruggles then assembled sixty-two pieces of artillery on west
side of Duncan Field and concentrated their fire upon Tuttle and the
batteries in his rear. At the same time Ruggles sent Wood, Anderson, and Stewart to reenforce Shaver in a renewed attack at the front.
While meeting this attack Tuttle was ordered at 5 p m. to withdraw
his biigade He gave personal direction to the Second and Seventh
Iowa and with them ietiied to the right of Huilbut's division, near
the siege guns, where he assumed command of the iemnant of the
Second Division and formed his line near the camp of the Fourteenth
Iowa. The staff officei sent by Tuttle to order the Twelfth and Fouiteenth Iowa to fall back directed the commanding officers of those
regiments to "about face and fall back slowly " Marching by the
rear rank about 200 yards, these regiments encountered Confederate
troops across their line of retreat. These they engaged and foiced
back to the camp of Hurlbut's First Brigade, wheie the Confedeiates
were ieenforced and the two iegiments, together with two from the
Third Brigade, and a part of Prentiss' division were surrounded and
captured at 5.30 p. m The Fourteenth Iowa suriendered to the
Ninth Mississippi of Chalmers' biigade, which had occupied the
extreme *right* of the Confederate army. The Twelfth Iowa surren-
deied to Colonel Looney, of the Thirty-eighth Tennessee, Pond's brigade, from the extreme *left* of the Confederate Army
    The Second and Seventh Iowa were with Tuttle's command on Mon-
day in reseive to General Ciittenden During the day the Second
Iowa was sent to ieenforce Nelson's left and in a charge across a field
defeated an attempt of the enemy to tuin the left of the Army of the
Ohio. Later the Seventh Iowa charged a battery in Crittenden's fiont.

Second Brigade

(McArthur's)

    This brigade, composed of five regiments, the Ninth and Twelfth
Illinois, Thirteenth and Fourteenth Missouri, and the Eighty-first
Ohio, was encamped on Hambuig and Savannah road near Snake
Creek. The first oider to the brigade Sunday morning, April 6, 1862,
disunited its regiments and sent them to different parts of the field,
and they were not united again until after the battle was over.
    The Thirteenth Missouri went to Sheiman; the Fourteenth Mis-
souri and Eighty-first Ohio to guard Snake Creek bridge. General

McArthur, with the Ninth and Twelfth Illinois and Willard's battery, moved directly south along the Hamburg road to the support of Colonel Stuart. Finding that Stuart had moved to the left rear of his camps, McArthur formed his command to Stuart's right rear just east of the Peach Orchard, the Ninth Illinois on the right next to Hamburg road; the Twelfth Illinois to its left; Willard's battery in rear of the Ninth. In this position McArthur sustained himself against Jackson's brigade until about 2 p. m., when Bowen from Reserve Corps was sent to reenforce Jackson. Under this combined attack McArthur was compelled to fall back. The Ninth Illinois, having lost 58 per cent of men engaged, retired to camp for ammunition and repairs. It was again engaged near its camp at 4.30 p m , and then joined Tuttle's command at the Fourteenth Iowa camp, and served with him on Monday. The Twelfth Illinois fell back to a second position where it joined the Fiftieth and Fifty-seventh Illinois and was engaged until about 4 p. m.. when it retired to its camp and passed the night On Monday it was engaged with McClernand's command

The Fourteenth Missouri was engaged Sunday in a skirmish with Brewer's cavalry on the right of Union line. On Monday it joined the Third Division and supported Thompson's battery. The Eighty-first Ohio remained on guard at Snake Creek bridge until 3 p. m. It then moved south to Hurlbut's headquarters, where it was engaged in the 4 30 conflict on Hamburg road. It bivouacked on McClernand's left Sunday night and served with Marsh's command on Monday. The Thirteenth Missouri joined McDowell's brigade on Sunday and was engaged with it in the conflict with Trabue at noon. It bivouacked Sunday night near Ninth Illinois camp and joined Sherman on Monday. General McArthur was wounded on Sunday and was succeeded in command by Colonel Morton, of the Eighty-first Ohio.

Third Brigade

(Sweeny's)

This brigade was composed of Eighth Iowa and the Seventh, Fiftieth, Fifty-second, Fifty-seventh, and Fifty-eighth Illinois It was encamped between the First and Second brigades and followed the First Brigade Sunday morning, April 6, 1862, on the Corinth road to the Eastern Corinth road, where it halted in reserve The Fifty-eighth and Seventh Illinois were at once moved forward to Duncan Field, where they formed at 9 30 a. m., on north side of the Corinth road, prolonging Tuttle's line and connecting with McClernand's left. Soon after, the Fiftieth Illinois was detached and sent to the left, where it became engaged on McArthur's left It fell back with the Twelfth Illinois to position east of the Bloody Pond, where it was joined at about 3 p m by the Fifty-seventh Illinois. These regiments held their position on left of the army until 4 p m , when they fell back and supported Stone's battery near the Landing in the last action of the day About noon the Eighth Iowa was put in line between Tuttle and Prentiss, where it supported Hickenlooper's battery until 5 p. m. The Fifty-second Illinois was sent, about 3 p. m., to the right. As it was moving down Tilghman Creek it ran into Wharton's cavalry, which was moving up the creek. A few volleys were exchanged by head of column, then the Fifty-second moved to the camp of the Fifteenth Illinois and was there engaged in repelling Pond's 4.30 p. m. attack. It

then retired to the siege guns. The Seventh and Fifty-eighth Illinois, on Tuttle's right, and the Eighth Iowa, on his left, participated in all the engagements described in the account of Tuttle's brigade until 4 p. m., when the Seventh retired to McClernand's seventh line. The Eighth Iowa and the Fifty-eighth Illinois were surrounded and captured at the same time that Prentiss was captured. Colonel Sweeny was wounded on Sunday and was succeeded on Monday by Colonel Baldwin, Fifty-seventh Illinois.

THIRD DIVISION

(Lew Wallace's.)

This division, composed of three brigades of infantry, two batteries of artillery, and two battalions of cavalry, was encamped north of Snake Creek; the First Brigade at Crump's Landing, the Second Brigade at Stony Lonesome; the Third Brigade at Adamsville Sunday morning, April 6, 1862, hearing sounds of battle up the river, General Wallace ordered his command to concentrate at Stony Lonesome, where at 11.30 a m , he received orders from General Grant, directing him to join the right of the army then engaged on the south side of Snake Creek. At 12 m , leaving two regiments and one gun to guard the public property at Crump's Landing, General Wallace started with his First and Second Brigades for the battlefield by the Shunpike road, which led to the right of Sherman's division as formed for battle in the morning.

At about 2 30 p m. a staff officer from General Grant overtook General Wallace on this road and turned him back to the river road, by which the Third Brigade having fallen into column, his division reached the battlefield after the action of Sunday was over

The division bivouacked in line of battle, facing west along the Savannah road north of McArthur's headquarters; the First Brigade on the left, with Thompson's battery on its right, the Second Brigade in the center; the Third Brigade on the right, with Thurber's battery at its center.

At daylight Monday morning, April 7, 1862, the batteries of the division engaged and dislodged Ketchum's Confederate battery, posted in the camp of the Eighth Illinois. At 6 30 a m , the division, its right on Owl Creek, advanced en échelon of brigades, left in front, crossed Tilghman Creek, and drove the Confederates from their position at Oglesby's headquarters. Then wheeling to the left against the left flank of the enemy, it advanced fighting, until at 4 p. m. it had pushed the Confederates through the Union camps and beyond Shiloh Branch. Near nightfall the division retired under orders to General Sherman's camps, where it bivouacked Monday night

First Brigade

(Smith's)

This brigade was encamped at Crump's Landing. It moved out 2½ miles on Purdy road to Stony Lonesome and joined the Second Brigade early Sunday morning, April 6, 1862 At 12 m , it started for Shiloh by a road leading southwesterly toward the right of Sherman's camps. At about 2.30 p m. the brigade was counter marched to the Adamsville and Pittsburg road by which it reached the battlefield about

52

dark and bivouacked in front of the camp of the Fourteenth Missouri.
On Monday the brigade formed in Perry Field, near McArthur's headquarters; the Twenty-fourth Indiana on the left, the Eleventh Indiana
on the right, and the Eighth Missouri in reserve   At about 6.30
a. m. it advanced across Tilghman Creek and at 8 a m entered the
field of Hare's brigade camp   It crossed said field in a southwesterly
direction, driving back the Confederate forces, thence through the
Cresent Field and to McDowell's brigade camp, where it bivouacked
Monday night   Losses during the day, 18 killed and 114 wounded.
The Twenty-fourth Indiana lost its lieutenant colonel, 1 captain, and 1
lieutenant killed.

Second Brigade.

(Thayer's)

This brigade consisting of Twenty-third Indiana, First Nebraska,
Fifty-eighth Ohio, and Sixty-eighth Ohio was encamped at Stony
Lonesome, 2¾ miles from the Tennessee River, on the Purdy road.
The Sixty-eighth Ohio was detailed to guard the baggage, the other
regiments of the brigade followed the First Brigade in its march
toward Shiloh April 6, 1862   It countermarched, from a point 4½
miles out, to the Adamsville and Pittsburg road, and thence via river
road to the battlefield, where it arrived after dark and bivouacked, in
line of battle, at the right of the First Brigade   Monday morning it
formed en échelon in right rear of the First Brigade, the First Nebraska
on the left, the Twenty-third Indiana on the right, and the Fifty-eighth
Ohio in reserve   It followed the movements of the First Brigade
through the day and bivouacked at night in the camp of the Forty-
sixth Ohio.

Third Brigade.

(Whittlesey's)

This brigade of four Ohio regiments, to wit, the Twentieth, Fifty-
sixth, Seventy-sixth, and Seventy-eighth, was encamped at Adams
ville, 4 miles from Crumps. It formed in line early Sunday morning,
April 6, 1862, when firing was heard at Shiloh, with all its camp equi-
page on wagons, and remained in line until 2 p m , when orders were
received to join the other brigades en route for Shiloh   It marched
on direct road toward Pittsburg, falling in behind the other brigades
as they came back into that road from the countermarch.   At about 4
p m the Fifty-sixth was detached and ordered to go with baggage to
Crumps Landing.   The other regiments arrived on the battlefield
after dark and bivouacked in front of the camp of the Eighty-first
Ohio.   Monday morning the brigade formed the extreme right of
Union line, its right, the Seventy-sixth, on the swamps of Owl Creek,
the Seventy-eighth on the left in rear of the right of the Second
Brigade, the Twentieth in reserve, until it crossed Tilghman Creek,
when it took position on the right   Retaining this formation the
brigade advanced, swinging to the left until 11 a. m., when it was
transferred to left of the division in support of Stuart's brigade of
Sherman's division.   The Seventy-sixth remained on the left, the
other regiments soon returned to the right, the Twentieth in front
line, the Seventy-eighth in reserve   The last engagement by this

brigade was between the Twentieth Ohio, in the field neal McDowell's headquaiters, aud Confederates at camp of Forty-sixth Ohio The brigade bivouacked in camp of Sixth Iowa Monday night

FOURTH DIVISION

(Hurlbut's)

This division, composed of three brigades of infantiy, three batteries of artillery, and two battalions of cavalry, arrived at Pittsburg Landing on boats March 16, 1862 On the 18th it disembarked and established its camps about 1 mile from the river, neai the point where the Hamburg and Savannah road crosses the road fiom Pittsburg to Corinth.

The division was formed about 8 a. m , Sunday morning, April 6, 1862, and soon after the Second Brigade was sent to reenforce General McClernand.

The First and Third Brigades, with the artillery, moved out to the support of Prentiss's division, but finding that Prentiss was falling back, Hurlbut put his division in line at the Peach Orchard field, the First Brigade on the south side, the Third Brigade on the west side, the batteries in the field. In this position he was attacked by Chalmers's and Gladden's brigades, which were following Prentiss's division, and by Robertson's, Harper's, and Girardey's batteries, which were stationed in Prentiss's camps A shell from one of these batteries blew up a caisson belonging to Myers's Thirteenth Ohio Battery; the men stampeded, abandoning their guns, and were not again in action at Shiloh.

Mann's battery fought with the division all day, and again on Monday Ross's battery did excellent service until ordeied to fall back at 4 p. m., and was preparing to ietire to the Landing when it was charged by Lindsay's Mississippi cavalry and captured. Only two guns were saved

Hurlbut held his position on two sides of the Peach Orchard until about 1 30 p m , when he was attacked by Breckinridge's corps Finding that Stuait was falling back on the left, Hurlbut ietired to the north side of the field with his First Brigade, and transferred his Third Brigade from the right to the left flank. Here he maintained himself until 3 p. m., when he was again obliged to retire to the left of his camps. About 4 p. m. he found that his left was again being turned and fell back to the siege guns and re-foimed The Second Brigade rejoined the division and all participated in the final action of the day. The division bivouacked in line of battle in front of the siege guns, and on Monday the First and Second Brigades and Mann's battery formed on McClernand's left; the Third Brigade repoited to Sheiman. All were engaged until the Confederates retired from the field.

First Brigade.

(Williams's)

This brigade of four regiments was encamped across the Corinth road, 1¼ miles from the river. On Sunday morning, April 6, 1862, at about 8 o'clock. it moved out on the Hamburg ioad and foimed line of battle along the south side of the Peach Orchard field in following

54

order from left to right: Forty-first Illinois, Twenty-eighth Illinois,
Thirty-second Illinois, Third Iowa. In this position it was attacked
by skirmishers from Chalmers's brigade and by artillery fire, by which
Colonel Williams was disabled and the command of the brigade passed
to Colonel Pugh, Forty-first Illinois Chalmers's brigade was withdrawn and Colonel Pugh retired his brigade to the center of the field,
where he was attacked at about 1.30 p m by Statham's and Stephen's
brigades, and at 2.30 was driven back to the north side of the field
The Thirty-second Illinois was transferred to the left of the brigade
east of Hamburg road, and lost its Lieutenant Colonel Ross, killed.
As the left of the line was driven back, Colonel Pugh again fell back
to the Wicker Field, where he held his line until 4 p. m , when the brigade retired, under Hurlbut's orders, to position near siege guns, where
it remained in line Sunday night The Third Iowa, occupying the
right of Hurlbut's line, connected with Prentiss and remained until
about 5 p. m., then retired through its camp and along Pittsburg road
just before the Confederates closed their line behind Prentiss. Major
Stone, commanding the regiment, was captured; other casualties of the
day among the officers left the regiment in command of Lieutenant
Crosley. He joined his command to the Thirteenth Iowa in the last
action of the day, and then reported to his brigade commander He
commanded the regiment, in action with his brigade, the next day
On Monday the brigade formed on McClernand's left and was
engaged until noon

Second Brigade.

(Veatch's)

This brigade, of four regiments, was encamped across the Hamburg
and Savannah road, north of the Corinth road. It was sent April 6,
1862, to reenforce McClernand, and moved out along the Corinth road
and formed in line behind Marsh's brigade at about 9 a m. in the following order from left to right Twenty-fifth Indiana, Fourteenth
Illinois, Forty-sixth Illinois, Fifteenth Illinois It became engaged at
about 10 30 a m., and at 11 a m. was compelled to retire. The Twenty-
fifth Indiana and Fourteenth Illinois fell back 200 yards, changing
front to rear on left companies, and formed along the road that runs
from review field past McClernand's headquarters A little later they
retired to the right of Hare's brigade, where they held their position
until after noon, when they fell back to McClernand's sixth line, where
they were engaged in Pond's repulse at 4 30 a m , after which they
joined Hurlbut in his last position on Sunday.

The Fifteenth Illinois lost all its field officers and several captains at first
position and retired at 11 a. m. to the Jones Field, where it was joined
by the Forty-sixth Illinois in supporting Barrett's battery. These two
regiments joined McDowell's left in the advance at 12 m. and continued
in line until 1 p m., when they retired—the Fifteenth Illinois to join
Hurlbut, the Forty-sixth Illinois to its camp for dinner, later the
Forty sixth joined Marsh's command on the Hamburg road and assisted
in the final action of the day and was with Marsh's command on Monday. The Fourteenth and Fifteenth Illinois and Twenty-fifth Indiana,
under Colonel Veatch, formed the left of the Army of the Tennessee
on Monday and joined McCook's right until about 11 a m., when they
crossed the Corinth road near Duncan's and were engaged in Review
field and in front line until 4 p m

Third Brigade.

(Lauman's)

This brigade had formeily belonged to the Army of the Ohio, where it was known as Cruft's brigade. It was sent from that army to reenforce Grant at Fort Donelson and had remained with the Army of the Tennessee General Lauman was assigned to the command April 5, 1862 Its camp was on the south side of Dill Branch, its right at the Hambuig ioad. About 8 a. m. Sunday, Apiil 6, 1862, it moved out to the west side of the Peach Orchard field and formed line with its right in the woods near the head of Tilghman Creek. The oider of its regiments from left to iight was Seventeenth Kentucky, Twenty-fifth Kentucky, Forty-fourth Indiana, Thirty-first Indiana About 9 a. m. it was attacked through the timber on its iight by Gladden's brigade, closely followed in succession by attacks, upon its whole line, by Stephens's brigade and the iight of Gibson's brigade One of the features of the battle at this place was the burning of the leaves and brush in the woods where the wounded weie lying.

About 2 p. m. the brigade was tiansferred to the left and formed in open woods just east of the Hamburg road, the Thirty-first Indiana in ieserve on left flank. This position was held until about 4 p m., when the brigade retired with its division to the seige guns. Aftei the action for the day had closed it moved 150 yards to front and bivouacked for the night On Monday at 10 a m it reported to Sherman and served with him until close of the battle.

FIFTH DIVISION.

(Sherman's)

This division, of four brigades of infantiy, three batteries of artillery, two battalions, and two independent companies of cavalry, was organized at Paducah about the 1st of March, 1862. It went up the Tennessee River to the mouth of Yellow Creek, and returned to Pittsbuig March 16, disembarked, and marched out to Monterey, returned to Pittsburg, and established its camps on the 19th along the Hamburg and Purdy road, its centei at Shiloh Church. On Sunday morning, April 6, 1862, the division formed in front of its camps wheie its Third and Fourth Brigades became engaged at 7.30 a. m These brigades, ieenfoiced by Raith's brigade of the First Division, held the line until 10 a m , when Sherman attempted to fall back to the Purdy road. In this movement his Third and Fourth Biigades became disorganized and ietiied to Hamburg and Savannah road, only paits of regiments iemaining in line McDowell's biigade, when ordered at 10 a. m. to fall back, became engaged in Crescent field and afterwards on McClernand's right until about 2 p. m.

Stuart's brigade was engaged with Chalmeis on the extreme left until 2 p. m Barrett's battery formed in front of Shiloh Church and opened fire at 7.30 a. m.; then at 10 a. m retired to Jones Field, where it was engaged until 2 p. m., when it retired to the river Waterhouse's batteiy went into action at 7 a. m. with two guns at Rhea House; these soon retired to main battery 150 yards in reai, where the full battery remained in action until 10 a m , when it was outflanked and lost three guns The remaindei of the battery retired disabled from the field.

Behr's battery was with McDowell's brigade, one gun guarding the bridge at Owl Creek   When Sherman ordered McDowell to join his other brigades near Shiloh Church, Captain Behr moved five guns down the road, and was directing them into battery when he was killed, his men stampeded, leaving the guns on the field.   The gun at Owl Creek served with McDowell in his first engagement, then retired.

On Monday Stuart's and Buckland's brigades were engaged on the left of Lew. Wallace all day.   Sherman was wounded on Sunday, but kept the field until the enemy retired on Monday.

First Brigade.

(McDowell's)

This brigade, of three regiments, was encamped on the Hamburg and Purdy road, its right on the high ground near Owl Creek, in the following order from left to right: Fortieth Illinois, Forty-sixth Ohio, Sixth Iowa.   At the first alarm Sunday morning, April 6, 1862, each regiment formed upon its color line.   Two companies of the Sixth Iowa, with one gun of Behr's battery, were on guard at the bridge over Owl Creek.   About 8 a. m. the brigade was advanced to the brow of the hill overlooking Shiloh Branch, the Fortieth Illinois joining the right of Buckland's brigade.   After a skirmish with Pond's brigade McDowell was ordered at 10 a. m. to retire to the Purdy road and move to the left to connect with Buckland's brigade near the cross-roads.   In obedience to this order the brigade abandoned its camps without a contest and moved by the left flank past McDowell's head-quarters, when it was discovered that the Confederates occupied the road between this brigade and Buckland's.   McDowell then moved directly north and put his brigade in line on west side of Crescent field, facing east, where he engaged and drove back the force of the enemy moving into said field   The brigade then moved northeasterly across Crescent Field and into Sowell Field, facing south, its left at Sowell house, where it connected with McClernand at 11 30 a. m , and advanced with him to the center of Marsh's brigade camp.   Here the Sixth Iowa was transferred from right to center of brigade, and Thirteenth Missouri placed between the Fortieth Illinois and Sixth Iowa, the Forty-sixth Ohio slightly in rear and to the extreme right of the line

At about 12 m. the brigade was attacked on its right flank by Trabue.   In an engagement lasting until 1 30 p m the Sixth Iowa had 52 killed—they were buried in one grave where they fell; the Forty-sixth Ohio had 246 killed and wounded, and the Fortieth Illinois 216 killed and wounded.   The brigade commander was thrown from his horse and disabled.   At 2 30 p. m the brigade retired to the Landing and later formed behind Hurlbut.   On Monday, the Sixth Iowa and Fortieth Illinois were attached to Garfield's brigade of Army of the Ohio, and remained with him until Wednesday, but were not engaged.

Second Brigade.

(Stuart's)

This brigade, of three regiments, was encamped at the junction of Hamburg and Purdy road with the Hamburg and Savannah road in the following order from left to right· Fifty-fifth Illinois, Fifty-fourth Ohio, Seventy-first Ohio, a company from each regiment on picket,

one at Lick Creek Ford, two on Bark road. These pickets gave warning, about 8 a. m. April 6, 1862, of the approach of the enemy.

Stuart formed his brigade on regimental color lines, but finding that he was exposed to artillery fire from batteries on bluff south of Locust Grove Creek, and obeying orders to guard Lick Creek Ford, he moved, at 10 a. m. to his left, placing the Fifty-fourth Ohio on his left behind McCullers field, the Fifty-fifth Illinois next to right, and the Seventy-first Ohio with its right behind the left of the Fifty-fifth Illinois camp. Chalmers placed his brigade in line on the bluff south of Locust Grove Creek, and, after clearing Stuart's camps with his artillery, moved across the creek and attacked the Fifty-fourth Ohio and Fifty-fifth Illinois in position. After a short conflict Stuart withdrew to a ridge running due east from his headquarters. The right, Seventy-first Ohio, occupying the buildings used as Stuart's headquarters, was here attacked by the right of Jackson's brigade and very soon retired, leaving a captain and 50 men prisoners. One part of the regiment under the major passed down a ravine to the Tennessee River, where they were picked up by a gunboat; another part retired to the Landing where they joined the brigade at night.

The Fifty-fourth Ohio and Fifty-fifth Illinois, with Stuart in command, successfully resisted the attacks of Chalmers until 2 p m., when their ammunition was exhausted and they were obliged to fall back to the Landing, where they reformed at the Log House, the Fifty-fourth Ohio in what is now the cemetery, the Fifty-fifth Illinois to its right supporting Silfversparre's battery, where they were engaged in resisting Chalmers' Sunday evening attack Stuart was wounded on Sunday, and was succeeded on Monday by Col. T. Kilby Smith, who, with the Fifty-fourth Ohio and Fifty-fifth Illinois, joined Sherman's command and fought on right next to Lew. Wallace all day.

Third Brigade

(Hildebrand's)

This brigade was encamped with its right, the Seventy-seventh Ohio, at Shiloh Church; its left, the Fifty-third Ohio, near the Rhea House and separated from the Fifty-seventh Ohio by a small stream with marshy margins. About 7 a. m. April 6, 1862, the brigade formed to meet the attack of the enemy, the Fifty-seventh and Seventy-seventh in advance of their camps in the valley of Shiloh Branch. The Fifty-third, being threatened by an attack in left flank, formed its line perpendicular to the left of its camp While in this position the brigade was attacked from the front by Cleburne's and Wood's brigades. This attack, falling upon the exposed flank of the Fifty-third, compelled it to change front to the rear on left company and form a new line in rear of its camp Attacked in this position, the regiment fell back disorganized, passing to the rear around the flank of the Forty-ninth Illinois, eight companies going to the Landing at once, two companies under the adjutant, E. C. Dawes, joining the Seventeenth Illinois The eight companies were reformed near the Landing by the major and supported Bouton's battery in McClernand's seventh line, and on Monday advanced with Marsh's command

The Fifty-seventh and Seventy-seventh were reinforced by Raith's brigade of the First Division and held their positions for some time, when they, too, fell back disorganized and were not again in line as regiments. Colonel Hildebrand acted as aid for General McClernand during Sunday.

Fourth Brigade.

(Buckland's)

This brigade was encamped with its left at Shiloh Church in the following order from left to right. Seventieth Ohio, Forty-eight Ohio, Seventy-second Ohio. It formed for battle Sunday morning April 6, 1862, about 200 yards in front of its camps, where it withstood the attacks of Cleburne, Anderson, and Johnson until 10 a. m. Its right flank was then threatened by Pond and Trabue and it was ordered to fall back to the Purdy road In making this movement the brigade was disorganized and scattered. The colonel of the Seventieth Ohio with a portion of his regiment joined the Third Brigade of McClernand's division and fell back with it to Jones Field, where it joined McDowell's brigade and was engaged with it until 1 p. m., when it retired to the Hamburg road. The adjutant and forty men of the Seventieth joined the Eleventh Illinois and fought with it until night. The Forty-eighth and Seventy-second retired to Hamburg and Savannah road, where Colonel Buckland reorganized his brigade and was engaged in the 4 30 p m affair, after which the Forty-eighth retired to the river for ammunition and spent the night in line near the log house, the Seventieth and Seventy-second passing the night in bivouac near McArthur's headquarters.

On Monday the brigade was reunited, and, with Stuart's brigade, formed Sherman's line that advanced to the right of McClernand's camps, thence southwesterly along the front of said camps to Shiloh Church, where the brigade reoccupied their camps at about 4 p m

SIXTH DIVISION

(Prentiss's)

On the 26th day of March, 1862, General Grant, by Special Order No 36, assigned General Prentiss to the command of unattached troops then arriving at Pittsburg Landing, with directions to organize these regiments, as they arrived upon the field, into brigades, and the brigades into a division, to be designated the Sixth Division.

Under this order one brigade of four regiments, commanded by Colonel Peabody, had been organized and was encamped on west side of the Eastern Corinth road, 400 yards south of the Barnes Field Another brigade, commanded by Colonel Miller, Eighteenth Missouri, was partially organized. Three regiments had reported and were in camp on the east side of the Eastern Corinth road Other regiments on their way up the river had been ordered to report to General Prentiss, but had not arrived

The Sixteenth Iowa arrived on the field on the 5th and sent its morning report to General Prentiss in time to have it included in his report of present for duty that day; it was not fully equipped and did not disembark from the boat until morning of the 6th The Fifteenth Iowa and Twenty-third Missouri arrived at the Landing Sunday morning, April 6, 1862. The Twenty-third Missouri reported to General Prentiss at his third position about 9.30 a m., and was placed in line at once as part of his command. The Fifteenth and Sixteenth Iowa were, by General Grant's order, sent to the right to reinforce McClernand. They reported to him at his fifth line in Jones Field, and were

hotly engaged from about 1 p m to 2.30 p. m.   Hickenlooper's Fifth
Ohio Battery and Munch's First Minnesota Battery and two battalions
of Eleventh Illinois Cavalry had been assigned to the division and
were encamped in rear of the infantry   One company from each regiment was on picket 1 mile in front of the camps.   On Saturday, April
5, a reconnoitering party under Colonel Moore, Twenty-first Missouri,
was sent out to the front.   Colonel Moore reported Confederate cavalry and some evidences of an infantry force in front, but he failed to
develop a regular line of the enemy. Prentiss doubled his pickets,
and at 3 a. m. Sunday sent out another party of three companies of
the Twenty-fifth Missouri, under Major Powell, to reconnoiter well to
the front.   This party encountered the Confederate picket under
Major Hardcastle in Fraley's field at 4 55 a m   These pickets at once
engaged, and continued their fire until about 6 30 a. m., when the
advance of the main line of Hardee's corps drove Powell back

General Prentiss, hearing the firing, formed his division at 6 a. m.
and sent Peabody's brigade in advance of his camp to relieve the retiring pickets and posted Miller's brigade 300 yards in front of his camp,
with batteries in the field at right and left of the Eastern Corinth road.
In this position the division was attacked at 8 a. m. by the brigades of
Gladden, Shaver, Chalmers, and Wood and driven back to its camp,
where the contest was renewed.   At 9 a. m. Prentiss was compelled to
abandon his camp and fall back to his third position, which he occupied at 9.05 a. m., in an old road between the divisions of Hurlbut and
W. H L. Wallace   Hickenlooper lost two guns in first position and
Munch had two disabled   Each brought four guns into line at the Hornets' Nest.   Prentiss was joined by the Twenty-third Missouri,
which gave him about 1,000 men at his third position.   With this
force he held his line against the attacks of Shaver, Stephens, and
Gibson, as described in account of Tuttle's brigade, until 4 p. m when
Hurlbut fell back and Prentiss was obliged to swing his division back
at right angles to Tuttle in order to protect the left flank   When Tuttle's left regiments marched to the rear Prentiss fell back behind them
towards the Corinth road and was surrounded and captured at 5.30
p m. near the forks of the Eastern Corinth road   Hickenlooper and
Munch withdrew just before they were surrounded, Hickenlooper
reporting to Sherman and becoming engaged in the 4.30 action on
Hamburg road   Munch's battery reported to Colonel Webster and
was in position at mouth of Dill Branch, where it assisted in repelling
last attack Sunday night.

First Brigade.

(Peabody's)

This brigade of four regiments was encamped on west side of Eastern Corinth road, about one-half mile south of Hamburg and Purdy
road, in the following order from left to right: Sixteenth Wisconsin,
Twenty-first Missouri, Twelfth Michigan, Twenty-fifth Missouri.
Three companies of the Twenty-fifth Missouri under its major, Powell,
were sent out at 3 a. m. April 6, 1862, to reconnoiter.   Moving southwest from camp, Powell passed between the Rhea and Seay fields
and into the main Corinth road, where one of Sherman's picket posts
was stationed   Beyond the picket, and near the southeast corner of
Fraley field, he encountered Confederate pickets, and was fired upon at

4 55 a. m. After an engagement of over an hour, Powell fell back before the advance of Wood's brigade to the Seay Field, where he was reinforced by Colonel Moore with his regiment, the Twenty-first Missouri, and four companies of the Sixteenth Wisconsin Colonel Moore took command, but was soon severely wounded, and Captain Saxe, Sixteenth Wisconsin, was killed. Lieutenant Colonel Woodyard, Twenty-first Missouri, assumed command, and was engaged about one hour, when he fell back to Rhea Field, where he was met by Colonel Peabody and the remainder of the brigade. Peabody held the Confederates in check until 8 a. m., when he fell back to his camp Here he was attacked by the brigade of Shaver and the right of Wood's brigade. Peabody was killed and the brigade forced to abandon its camp at 9 a. m. The brigade organization was broken up, a part retiring through McClernand's lines and about 200 of the Twenty-first Missouri and 100 of the Twelfth Michigan joining Prentiss at his third position, where they were surrounded and most of them captured at 5 30 p. m Sunday afternoon.

Second Brigade.

(Miller's)

This brigade had three regiments in camp—a fourth assigned and reported but not yet in camp. The regiments were encamped between the Eastern Corinth road and Locust Grove in the following order from left to right: Eighteenth Wisconsin, Sixty-first Illinois, Eighteenth Missouri. The Sixteenth Iowa arrived at the Landing on Saturday, April 5, 1862. The colonel reported for duty and handed in his morning report, so that his regiment is included in Miller's report of present for duty. Not being fully equipped, the regiment did not go to camp, but remained at Landing; on Sunday it, with Fifteenth Iowa, was, by order of General Grant, held for a time near the Landing to stop stragglers, and then sent to reinforce McClernand at his fourth line, where they were engaged and lost heavily.

The Eighteenth Wisconsin arrived on the field on Saturday afternoon and went at once into camp, but did not get into the morning report of that day and are not included in Miller's present for duty. The brigade was formed for battle Sunday morning at 6 o'clock 300 yards in front of its camp, at south side of Spain Field, where it was attacked by Gladden and Chalmers at 8 a m. and was driven back into camp, and at 9 a m was compelled to abandon its camp Parts of the Eighteenth Wisconsin and Eighteenth Missouri, about 300 men, formed with Prentiss at his third position and remained with him until captured at 5.30 p. m. The Sixty-first Illinois passed beyond or through Hurlbut's line and was in reserve behind that division all day Sunday, except about an hour when it relieved another regiment in front line.

UNASSIGNED.

The Fifteenth Michigan arrived at Pittsburg Landing April 6, 1862. Arms had been issued to the men, but no ammunition had been supplied. The regiment moved out upon the field early Sunday morning and formed line and stacked knapsacks, at the left of the Eighteenth Wisconsin in Locust Grove, just as Chalmers appeared in front and moved to the attack. Failing to obtain ammunition, Colonel Oliver

ordered his men to fix bayonets, as if to charge the approaching Confederates, but reconsidered and about faced his men and returned to the Landing, where he obtained ammunition and again joined the fighting line at some place not now determined On Monday morning the regiment joined Rousseau's brigade of the Army of the Ohio and fought with conspicuous gallantry all day.

The Fourteenth Wisconsin arrived upon the field Sunday night, and on Monday joined Smith's brigade of the Army of the Ohio and served with it all day. It assisted in the capture of a battery, one gun of which was awarded to this regiment and sent to the State of Wisconsin.

Silfversparre's battery (H), First Illinois, arrived upon the field Sunday, April 6. Its guns were four 20-pounder Parrotts. Horses had not been supplied. The men got the guns up the bank and placed them in battery in front of the Log House, where they were engaged Sunday evening.

Bouton's battery (I), First Illinois, arrived at Pittsburg Sunday morning fully equipped, but without drill, and with horses that had never been harnessed to a gun The battery was taken ashore and reported to Sherman, and rendered good service in repelling last attack upon his line at 4 30 p. m. It remained with Sherman on Monday all day, and received special mention by Colonel Gibson of the Army of the Ohio.

Siege guns.—Battery B, Second Illinois. The guns belonging to this battery were, under the direction of Colonel Webster, gotten ashore Sunday afternoon and placed in position one-fourth of a mile west of the Log House, where they formed a rallying point for all troops coming back from the front.

Powell's battery (F), Second Illinois, was encamped near the landing awaiting an assignment which Captain Powell understood would place him in McClernand's division After waiting some time on Sunday morning for orders, Powell attempted to take his battery to McClernand.   He moved out along the Corinth road, passing through Sweeny's troops at east side of Duncan field and arriving near the Duncan House, after Hare's brigade had fallen back, found himself, suddenly, in close proximity to the Confederate line of battle In retiring one gun was upset and left just behind the Duncan Field With five guns Powell reported to W. H. L. Wallace near the left of his line, where he was engaged until about 5 o'clock, when Captain Powell was wounded and his battery retired to its camp, where it was engaged at 6 p. m. in the final action of Sunday

Margraf's, Eighth, Ohio Battery arrived at the Landing the last of March. By an order issued April 2 it had been assigned to the Third Division, but had not reported to that division. The only official report of its action is given in the report of the First Minnesota, which says that the "Eighth Ohio was on its left in the action of 6 p. m., Sunday, at the mouth of Dill Branch."

ARMY OF THE OHIO

Soon after the consolidation of the Departments of the Ohio and Missouri, General Halleck ordered General Buell to move his army from Nashville to Savannah, Tenn., and form junction with the Army of the Tennessee. Upon General Buell's suggestion to march his army across the country rather than transfer it by boats, it was so

ordered, and General Buell with the advance of his army reached Savannah, Tenn., April 5, 1862 Early Sunday, April 6, General Grant informed General Buell by note [a] of the situation at Shiloh and ordered General Nelson [b] to march his division up the east side of the Tennessee to a point opposite Pittsburg Landing, where boats would be found to ferry him across the river. General Buell and staff reached Pittsburg Landing by boat between 2 and 3 o'clock Ammen's brigade, the advance of Nelson's division, arrived upon the field at about 5 30 p. m., a part of it engaging in the repulse of the Confederates in the last attack of Sunday During the night the remainder of Nelson's division and Crittenden's division arrived on the field, and early Monday morning two brigades of McCook's division reached the Landing.

In the action of the 7th the Army of the Ohio occupied the left of the Union line, extending in a semicircle from the Tennessee River, south of Dill Branch, to north side of the Corinth road 1 mile from the Landing, Nelson's division on the left, Crittenden in the center, McCook on the right. "The enemy on a line slightly oblique to ours and beyond open fields with a battery in front of Nelson's left, a battery in front of Crittenden's left, a battery in front of Crittenden's right and McCook's left and another battery in front of McCook's right A short distance in rear of the enemy's left were the encampments of McClernand's and Sherman's divisions, which the enemy held. While troops were getting into position, Mendenhall's battery engaged the enemy's second battery with some effect. Bartlett's battery engaged the enemy's third battery." [c]

The divisions of the Army of the Ohio moved forward preserving their relative positions in line and became engaged about 8 a. m. They advanced slowly until about 2 p. m., when Wood's division arrived just as the final retreat of the Confederates began. In the forward movement McCook's division kept the main Corinth road, Crittenden's division about the direction of the eastern Corinth road. This separated these divisions so that at about 11 a. m. Veatch and Tuttle, from the Army of the Tennessee, were moved into the interval between McCook and Crittenden and became engaged in the Review field At 4 p m the Confederates had retired from the field, and the Army of the Ohio bivouacked on a line extending from Stuart's camps through Prentiss's camps to near Shiloh Church.

Terrill's battery (H), Fifth United States, belonging to McCook's division, was detached for service with Nelson and was in action on Hamburg road and at the Peach Orchard.

FOURTH DIVISION.

(Nelson's)

The head of this division arrived opposite to Pittsburg Landing about 5 p. m., April 6, 1862. One brigade, Ammen's, crossed the river and parts of the Thirty-sixth Indiana and Sixth Ohio were engaged in the closing action of Sunday. At 9 p. m. the entire division had crossed the Tennessee River and formed along the north side of Dill Branch, where it bivouacked Sunday night with pickets across the branch. At 5 30 a m on the 7th the division advanced and at 7 a. m. formed on south side of the branch and awaited the completion of the

line   At 8 a. m. it attacked the Confederates in the Peach Orchard. Mendenhall's battery with the right and Terrill's battery with the left. The division gained the south side of the Peach Orchard at 2 p m., the Confederates retiring. This closed the conflict on the left. The division remained in line until night and bivouacked with its left in Stuart's camps, its right near Prentiss's headquarters.

Tenth Brigade

(Ammen's)

This brigade, composed of the Thirty-sixth Indiana and the Sixth and Twenty-fourth Ohio, crossed the Tennessee River at 5.30 p m , Sunday, April 6, 1862.   Eight companies of the Thirty-sixth Indiana and four companies of the Sixth Ohio were formed one-quarter of a mile in front of the Log House in support of Stone's battery, "the left in a ravine parallel with the Tennessee River and having water in it."   These companies participated in the final repulse of the Confederates Sunday night.   The Twenty-fourth Ohio was sent one-half mile to the right, but did not become engaged.   After the repulse of the enemy the brigade formed 300 yards in advance on the crest of the bluffs of Dill Branch, where it bivouacked Sunday night.   On Monday it formed line of battle with the Thirty-sixth Indiana on the left, the Sixth Ohio on the right, and the Twenty-fourth Ohio in reserve, and at 5.30 a. m. crossed the ravine and at 8 a. m., became engaged on the extreme left of the Union line, near Tennessee River   At about 11 a. m. Ammen's advance was checked by an attempt of Confederates to turn his left. He was reinforced by Second Iowa and another regiment and repulsed the attack. He reached Stuart's camp at about 1 p. m., but was driven back   At 2 p. m. this camp was again taken, the Confederates retiring from this part of the field.

Nineteenth Brigade.

(Hazen's)

This brigade reached the battlefield at 9 p m., April 6, 1862, and bivouacked, on the right of the division, south of the siege-gun battery, in the following order: Ninth Indiana on the left, Sixth Kentucky on the right, and the Forty-first Ohio in reserve. The brigade advanced at 5.30 a m., April 7, and became engaged about 8 a. m at Wicker Field. The Ninth Indiana lost heavily at the house on the north side of the Peach Orchard. The brigade then advanced to the Wheat Field, where a battery was captured and its guns spiked by the Forty-first Ohio This advanced position was held only a few minutes, the brigade falling back somewhat disorganized to Wicker Field, from which it advanced at 2 p m. across the west side of Peach Orchard and took position near Prentiss's headquarters. It was not again engaged, and bivouacked there Monday night.

Twenty-second Brigade.

(Bruce's)

This brigade arrived at Pittsburg Landing about 6 o'clock Sunday evening, April 6, 1862. It bivouacked between the Tenth and Nineteenth Brigades, the Second Kentucky on the left, the First Kentucky on the right, and the Twentieth Kentucky in reserve.

It held the center of the division all day and was engaged in a charge across the Peach Orchard, in which a battery was captured and lost again. At 2 p. m the enemy retired and this brigade took position on south side of Peach Orchard, where it bivouacked Monday night.

FIFTH DIVISION

(Crittenden's)

This division, consisting of the Eleventh and Fourteenth Brigades and Mendenhall's and Bartlett's batteries, came from Savannah on boats, arriving at Pittsburg Landing during the night of Sunday, April 6, 1862, and bivouacked along the Corinth road in the rear of Nelson's division. Early Monday morning it moved out and formed line in front of the camps of the Thirty-second and Forty-first Illinois, joining Nelson's right, the Fourteenth Brigade in front line, the Eleventh Brigade in reserve. At about 8 a. m. the division advanced and soon after became engaged at the position held by Prentiss and Tuttle on Sunday. Bartlett's battery on the right near the fork of the Eastern Corinth road was engaged until 12 noon, when it retired to the Landing for ammunition. Mendenhall's battery was engaged on Nelson's right until after noon, when it took position in rear of the Fifth Division and was there engaged until the close of action.

The division was engaged along the Eastern Corinth road and east of Duncan Field about four hours, in which time both brigades and all its regiments were repeatedly engaged. It advanced, capturing some guns, was repulsed and driven back to the road several times. At about 2 p. m. it gained and held the Hamburg and Purdy road, which ended the fighting on this part of the line. It bivouacked Monday night in front of Prentiss's camps.

Eleventh Brigade.

(Boyle's)

This brigade formed in rear of the Fourteenth Brigade at 8 a m. Monday, April 7, 1862, near Hurlbut's headquarters, in the following order from left to right. Ninth Kentucky, Thirteenth Kentucky, Nineteenth Ohio, the Fifty-ninth Ohio in reserve. At about 10 a. m it became engaged at the east side of Duncan Field, the Nineteenth Ohio in front of Bartlett's battery. The brigade relieved the Fourteenth Brigade and was engaged on the front line in two or three engagements and finally took position on right of the Fourteenth and held it until night. The Nineteenth Ohio was at 12 m. sent to the support of Nelson's division and was engaged at the Peach Orchard

Fourteenth Brigade.

(Smith's)

This brigade formed in front of the camps of the Thirty-second and Forty-first Illinois at 8 a. m. Monday, April 7, 1862, in the following order. Thirteenth Ohio on the left, Twenty-sixth Kentucky on the right, and the Eleventh Kentucky in reserve. The Fourteenth Wisconsin was attached temporarily to the brigade and placed on the right

65

of the Twenty-sixth Kentucky. It served with the brigade all day. The brigade advanced, with its right on Eastern Corinth road, and became engaged along the sunken road, where Tuttle and Prentiss fought on Sunday It advanced through the thick brush and assisted in the capture of a battery in the Wheat Field, but was obliged to abandon it and return to old road In the final action about 2 p. m it captured some guns of another battery, which were successfully held as trophies by the brigade

SECOND DIVISION.

(McCook's)

The advance of this division, Rousseau's brigade, reached Pittsburg Landing Monday morning, April 7, 1862, and took its place in line of battle at 8 a. m. on Crittenden's right Kirk's brigade formed in rear of Rousseau. These brigades were joined by Gibson's about noon The advance of the division was along the Corinth road to the Water Oaks Pond, where it was engaged at noon Its last engagement was at Sherman's headquarters, from which point the Confederates retired from the field.

Terrell's battery belonging to this division was engaged on Nelson's left until 2 p. m., when it moved toward the right and engaged a battery in McCook's front

Fourth Brigade.

(Rousseau's)

This brigade formed in line of battle on Crittenden's right at 8 a. m., April 7, 1862, in front of the camp of the Third Iowa, in the following order: Sixth Indiana on the left, First Ohio in the center, First Battalions of Nineteenth, Fifteenth, and Sixteenth United States Infantry on the right, and the Fifth Kentucky in reserve. The Fifteenth Michigan was attached temporarily to this brigade and served with it all day. At 9 a. m. the brigade advanced across Tilghman Creek and engaged Trabue's brigade until about 11 a. m., when Trabue retired and Rousseau advanced to Woolf Field, where he found a force of the enemy on its west side. His ammunition being exhausted, Rousseau retired and Kirk's brigade took his place in the first line. As soon as ammunition was supplied Rousseau took position again in the front line and engaged the enemy until he retired from the field

Fifth Brigade

(Kirk's)

This brigade was in rear of Rousseau until about noon, when it relieved that brigade and formed in front line behind the Water Oaks Pond in following order: Thirty-fourth Illinois on the left, Thirtieth Indiana in the center, and the Twenty-ninth Indiana on the right; the Seventy-seventh Pennsylvania detached to the left, where it was twice charged by cavalry. Later in its advance the Seventy-seventh captured Colonel Battle, Twentieth Tennessee. The Thirty-fourth Illinois in the first advance passed directly through Water Oaks Pond.

Its commander, Major Levanway, was killed, and Colonel Kirk, commanding the brigade, was wounded. The engagement here was the last effort of the Confederates to hold their line, and closed the fighting for the day

Sixth Brigade.

(Gibson's)

This brigade arrived upon the field about noon and joined its division at Woolf Field, and was at once ordered into line on Kirk's left, where it became engaged at once The Thirty-second Indiana was detached and is mentioned in the reports as having made a bayonet charge in front of Kirk's brigade near the Pond. It followed the retiring Confederates until ordered to return It failed to find its division and bivouacked by itself Monday night. The other regiments of the brigade bivouacked near the camp of the Fourth Illinois Cavalry.

SIXTH DIVISION

(Wood's)

This division arrived upon the field about 2 p. m. It was ordered into line on Crittenden's right. When it got into position the battle was about over, and only Wagner's brigade became engaged, and that only for a few minutes, the Fifty-seventh Indiana having four men wounded. The division bivouacked in rear of the right of Prentiss's division camps.

THE ARMY OF THE MISSISSIPPI (CONFEDERATE)

This army assembled near Corinth, Miss It was organized into four army corps and commenced its movements toward Pittsburg April 3, 1862, under General Order No. 8, which directed the Third Corps, Major General Hardee, to move from Corinth by Ridge road to near Mickey's, at the intersection of the Ridge road with road from Monterey to Savannah, the Second Corps, Major General Bragg, to assemble at Monterey and move thence to the Ridge road near Mickey's, in two columns, the left wing by the Purdy and the right wing by the Savannah road, falling in behind Hardee's corps; the First Corps, Major General Polk, to assemble at Mickey's, taking the road behind Bragg's corps; Ruggles's division coming from Corinth by the Ridge road; Cheatham's division from Bethel and Purdy; the Reserve Corps, Brigadier General Breckinridge, to assemble at Monterey, from Burnsville, and follow Bragg's corps to Mickey's and fall in behind Polk's corps; the cavalry to deploy on the flanks guarding Lick Creek fords on the right and the road to Stantonville on the left.

The order contemplated an attack upon the Union camps near Pittsburg Landing at sunrise Saturday morning, April 5, but on account of bad roads and other delays the several corps were not in position assigned them until nearly dark on Saturday, and the attack was deferred until Sunday morning, April 6 The army bivouacked Saturday night in order of battle, the Third Corps in the front line across the Pittsburg Landing road one-half mile in advance of the forks of the Bark road; the Second Corps 800 yards in rear of the first line; the First Corps in column of brigades in rear of the second line; the Reserve Corps 1 mile in rear on the road to Mickey's.[a]

_____

a 10 War Records, 614

General Johnston established his headquarters at the forks of the old Bark and Pittsburg roads.

The forward movement to the attack commenced at about sunrise Sunday morning, April 6, General Johnston in person accompanying the right, Gladden's and Shaver's brigades,[a] until the first camp was attacked He then rode to the left, where Cleburne's brigade was advancing to the attack,[a] and from there conducted Stewart's brigade to the right He then, from the camp of the Eighteenth Wisconsin, directed the movements of Chalmers's and Jackson's brigades[b] to the right, while Hardee, who was with him here,[c] was directing Shaver, Wood, and Stewart to the left. General Johnston then ordered the reserve corps forward, and at 12.30 was placing these troops in position south of the Peach Orchard, and at his staff occupying for over an hour a position due south of the center of the Peach Orchard, on the left bank of Locust Grove Creek.[d] From this point he went forward behind Bowen's brigade, and was killed near the southeast corner of the Peach Orchard at 2 30 p m. His body was carried to Corinth that afternoon and was buried at New Orleans, La.

Gen G. T. Beauregard, second in command, and commanding the army after 2.30 p m., had his headquarters Saturday night at the present forks of Bark and Pittsburg roads.[e] At 10 a. m Sunday morning the general and his staff moved forward to within one-half mile of the camps (near Plum Orchard Hospital, according to Captain Irwin). About noon he moved up to the Rhea House and at 2 p m. forward to the crossroads near Water Oaks Pond. Here he received information of the death of General Johnston and assumed command of the army. At night his headquarters was established at General Sherman's tent, near Shiloh Church From this point he directed the battle on Monday. When he directed the army to retire he personally placed a brigade and several pieces of artillery in position on the first ridge south of Shiloh Branch, a battery at Wood's house and Breckinridge's corps on the high ground near Bark Road, and then with his staff retired to Corinth via Monterey.

THIRD CORPS

(Hardee's)

This corps, consisting of three brigades, formed the first line of battle just behind Wood's field and cotton press. The three brigades not filling all the space desired, Gladden's brigade from Bragg's corps was added to the right and placed under Hardee's orders. The corps in line of battle had its center on, and perpendicular to, the Pittsburg road, its left near Owl Creek, its right across the Bark road, in the following order of brigades from left to right· Cleburne's Second Brigade, Wood's Third Brigade, Shaver's First Brigade, and Gladden's brigade Gen. T. C Hindman was intrusted with the command of his own and Wood's brigade, and is, in a few cases, referred to as commanding a division He remained with his old brigade—the First—and does not appear to have given any orders to Wood, and is, in nearly every case, referred to as commanding a brigade. He was dis-

[a] 10 War Records. 403
[b] 10 War Records, 532, 554, 558
[c] 10 War Records, 569
[d] Statement of Senator Harris
[e] 10 War Records, 401.

abled about 11 a. m. on the 6th, near the northeast corner of the Review field. The Third Corps in its advance from Mickey's had a skirmish on Friday in which a few prisoners were taken on both sides; another engagement with a picket post near Howell's on Saturday, and on Sunday morning the picket of this corps, under Major Hardcastle, stationed at the corner of Fraley's and Wood's fields, was attacked at 4.55 a. m. by a reconnoitering party sent out by General Prentiss. This affair between pickets lasted over an hour, the corps in the meantime getting into line and advancing, driving back the reconnoitering party, and following it to the first line of camps, where the battle became general.

General Hardee in person moved with the right of his line, where General Johnston was directing the battle, until the first camps were passed, when Hardee, after consulting with Johnston at the camp of the Eighteenth Wisconsin, went to the left[a] and took general direction of the left flank of the army the remainder of the day.

On Monday he was in command on the extreme right of the line.[b] His corps remained intact until about 9 a m. of the 6th, when his troops intermingled with other troops With the possible exception of two or three regiments of Cleburne's brigade, none of his corps were under his command on Sunday after he moved to the left. Neither of his brigade organizations were under his command on Monday Under General Beauregard's orders, Hardee commenced the withdrawal of his troops at 1 p m. Monday.

Third Brigade.

(Wood's)

This brigade consisted of five regiments and two battalions of infantry, one battery of artillery, and one company of cavalry. It occupied the center of Hardee's line of battle Saturday night, its right on the Corinth and Pittsburg road, in the following order from left to right: Twenty-seventh Tennessee, Sixteenth Alabama, Forty-fourth Tennessee, Ninth Arkansas, Eighth Arkansas, Fifty-fifth Tennessee; the Third Mississippi on picket, and Harper's (Mississippi) battery in rear of the infantry. Major Hardcastle with the Third Mississippi, on picket at the corner of two fields one-fourth mile in advance of the main line, was attacked at 4 55 Sunday morning by a reconnoitering party sent out by General Prentiss. Hardcastle fought the party until 6.30,[c] when the brigade advanced to his support and following the reconnoitering party moved directly forward to the attack of the Union camps, which it reached at 9 a m [d] In this movement Wood's brigade was guide for first line [e] The left of Wood's brigade struck the front of the Fifty-third Ohio camp, its right extending into the camps of Peabody's brigade. The left wing, Twenty-seventh Tennessee, by a movement to the right, avoided the camp of the Fifty-third Ohio, which was being swept by the fire of Waterhouse's battery, while the right passed directly through a part of Peabody's camp, pressing the Union forces back until Wood's left had passed Waterhouse's battery and become exposed to a left flank and rear fire [f] and the right had reached a field in the rear of Peabody's camp. Here the brigade wheeled to the left and attacked the second line of camps to the rear

---

[a] 10 War Records, 404, 569	[d] 10 War Records, 596
[b] 10 War Records, 534	[e] 10 War Records, 580
[c] 10 War Records, 603	[f] 10 War Records, 591,

of the battery [a] (Raith's brigade camps). After making left wheel and adjusting his line by bringing the Ninth and Eighth Arkansas to the left flank—making his line from left to right Ninth Arkansas, Eighth Arkansas, Twenty-seventh Tennessee, Sixteenth Alabama, Forty-fourth Tennessee, Fifty-fifth Tennessee, and Third Mississippi—Wood moved directly forward, doubling up the left of Raith's brigade and attacking McClernand's Second Brigade on the Corinth road, where he captured Burrows's battery. In this attack General Wood was thrown from his horse and disabled so that he left the field until 2 30 p m The brigade was disorganized and did not again act together during the day The Twenty-seventh Tennessee rested from 10.50 until 3 p. m , then joined Wood when he resumed command The Sixteenth Alabama and the Fifty-fifth Tennessee joined Shaver's brigade in its movement to the right under General Stewart [b] and then, with the Third Mississippi, went to the rear with the prisoners,[c] returning to the field Monday morning.

The Forty-fourth Tennessee became separated from the brigade during the charge and fought to the right of Shaver's brigade in Hornets' Nest [d] It joined Wood again at 3 o'clock. The Eighth Arkansas and the Ninth Arkansas rested an hour, then after 12 m joined Cleburne's and Shaver's forces in an attack at Duncan House.[e] and at 3 o'clock joined General Wood. The Third Mississippi joined Colonel Vaughan but was not engaged; it joined the Sixteenth Alabama and Fifty-fifth Tennessee as guard for the prisoners, and returned to the field on Monday. Harper's battery became detached Sunday morning and was engaged with Shaver's brigade, and in the afternoon with General Cheatham at Peach Orchard. Avery's Georgia Dragoons went to the right as guard at Green's Ford

At 2 30 p. m. on Sunday General Wood resumed command and brought together four regiments, the Twenty-seventh Tennessee, Eighth Arkansas, Ninth Arkansas, and the Forty-fourth Tennessee, and reported to General Ruggles west of Duncan House. At 4 o'clock he was sent with General Anderson to the right to attack the Union force at Hornets' Nest He did not become engaged but followed the retiring troops of Tuttle's brigade, and after the surrender moved toward the front and center near the present schoolhouse At sunset [f] he moved back to one of the encampments in the rear.

Monday morning he formed the remnant of the four regiments, not over 650 men,[g] and went into action on south end of Jones Field At 11 a m he fell back to Shiloh Church, and soon after moved to the right and made a charge at the Water Oaks Pond, where he engaged McCook's division and the left of Sherman's command. He then retired to high ground south of Shiloh Branch Harper's battery was on the right Monday. The Third Mississippi joined Wood on Monday near Shiloh Church.

First Brigade

(Shaver's)

This brigade formed line of battle Saturday on Wood's right, its line extending from Pittsburg road to Bark road in following order from left to right: Seventh Arkansas, Second Arkansas, Sixth Arkansas,

---

[a] 10 War Records, 605
[b] 10 War Records, 597
[c] 10 War Records, 592, 593, 608.
[d] 10 War Records, 608.

[e] 10 War Records, 582, 599, 601, 603
[f] 10 War Records, 593
[g] 10 War Records, 594.

Third Confederate, Swett's (Mississippi) battery in the rear. The Fifth Arkansas and Miller's (Tennessee) battery are included with this brigade in " Organization of the army," but are not again mentioned in reports.

The brigade moved forward at 6 30 a. m Sunday meeting with little resistance until within one-half mile of the Union camps Here Swett's and Harper's [a] batteries took position on the right near Eastern Corinth road and engaged the Union batteries (Hickenlooper's and Munch's). A charge was ordered and Peabody's camp was captured and his men pursued to a ravine and to an old field (Barnes's). The Third Confederate continuing the pursuit beyond the ravine became detached from its brigade and was engaged at Hornets' Nest soon after 9 a. m Colonel Shaver reorganized his command and was ordered to make change of front to the left, in conjunction with Wood's left wheel, to attack a camp (Raith's) Before completing the movement he was ordered to reform and move by left flank one-half mile [a] to an old farm, from which he attacked the enemy (Hare's brigade) behind a large field. The left regiments passed through this field, driving back Hare's brigade and occupying the ground one and one-half [b] hours. The right of the brigade passed to the right of the Review field and became engaged with Sweeny's and Tuttle's brigades and was exposed to a heavy cross fire from the Union batteries in the rear of Tuttle. Swett's battery took position on Shaver's right and engaged those batteries. General Hindman was disabled by the fall of his horse and General Stewart took command of Hindman's troops, consisting of Shaver's brigade and the Sixteenth Alabama and Fifty-fifth Tennessee of Wood's brigade, and placing the Fourth Tennessee on the left of Shaver moved directly east from the northwest corner of Review field to Duncan House and attacked the troops behind Duncan Field Stewart was repulsed, and Shaver's brigade retired about 1 mile to a camp to replenish ammunition Between 2 and 3 o'clock Shaver's brigade made another attack at the Hornets' Nest and was again repulsed In this charge Lieutenant Colonel Dean, Seventh Arkansas, was killed within 50 paces of the front of the Fourteenth Iowa. The brigade then fell back and was not again engaged on Sunday. It retired a little farther to the rear and bivouacked for the night. On Monday the brigade formed on the Bark road. After some time the Second and Sixth Arkansas advanced to the left with General Cheatham, where an attack was made about 12 m and some guns captured, but were soon retaken, and the Confederates driven back in disorder. In attempting to rally his force Colonel Shaver was rendered senseless by the explosion of a shell near him, and his command disorganized The Seventh Arkansas was in support of a battery on Monday and later in the day became engaged on the right. The Third Confederate was detached to the right on Monday Swett's (Mississippi) battery, after its participation in the attack at Hornets' Nest on Sunday, was placed by General Ruggles in line of batteries on the east side of Review field, where it was supported by the One hundred and fifty-fourth Tennessee. No record of Swett's battery in engagement on Monday '

---

[a] 10 War Records, 669   [b] 10 War Records, 576

Second Brigade.

(Cleburne's)

This brigade formed the left of Hardee's line, in the following order from left to right: Second Tennessee (Bate), Twenty-fourth Tennessee, Fifth Tennessee (Hill), Sixth Mississippi, Twenty-third Tennessee, the Fifteenth Arkansas in advance as pickets and skirmishers, Shoup's battalion of artillery, consisting of Calvert's, Trigg's, and Hubbard's Arkansas batteries, in rear of the infantry. The left of the brigade was near Widow Howell's The advance was begun at 6.30 a. m., Sunday, and at about 8 a. m. the brigade became engaged along Shiloh Branch, its batteries on high ground in the rear. Its progress was impeded by the marshy ground and briers of the branch. After passing these obstructions, the right—Sixth Mississippi and the Twenty-third Tennessee—charged through the camp of the Fifty-third Ohio, but were repulsed by the fire of Waterhouse's battery and the infantry of Raith's and Hildebrand's brigades. The Twenty-third Tennessee was rallied with difficulty, but the Sixth Mississippi renewed the attack with vigor, and charged again and again, until it lost 300 men out of 425 engaged The left of the brigade met a like defeat in attempting to charge the position of Buckland's brigade and Barrett's battery, and was unable to advance until reinforced by Anderson's brigade from Bragg's corps,[a] and by Russell's and Johnson's brigades from Polk's corps. With these reinforcements Cleburne rallied 60 men of the Sixth Mississippi and about half of the Twenty-Third Tennessee and, in conjunction with troops from the other brigades, advanced along the Pittsburg Landing road to the point where Burrows's battery was captured, where he was joined by the Eighth Arkansas. With the fragments of these three regiments, Cleburne joined General Stewart at 12, noon, in an attack upon position at Duncan House, where some of Cleburne's men were taken prisoners by the Seventh Illinois. At 12 30 p. m , the Sixth Mississippi retired from the field, and the Twenty-third Tennessee was ordered to the rear to reorganize. Cleburne then went in search of the other regiments of his brigade and, at 3 p. m., found the Fifth and Twenty-fourth Tennessee and Fifteenth Arkansas resting under the brow of a hill, where they were soon joined by the Twenty-third Tennessee. The Fifth Tennessee, Twenty-fourth Tennessee, and Fifteenth Arkansas had advanced through Buckland's camp at about 10 a. m., and had joined Pond and Trabue,[b] and with them were engaged at 12 m. to 2.30 p m in front of Marsh's brigade camp, and had passed to rear of that camp when found by Cleburne. Colonel Bate, of the Second Tennessee, was wounded in front of Buckland's brigade, and the regiment was somewhat disorganized and was not again engaged on Sunday. On Monday, the Second Tennessee was engaged on the right under General Stewart. When Cleburne joined his left wing at 3 p. m. on Sunday, he advanced to the east side of Tilghman Creek, where he was engaged at 4.30 p. m in the attack upon McClernand's sixth line. He then moved forward until he came under fire of the artillery and gunboats, where he halted until dark, when he was ordered to the rear and retired to a camp near the Bark

---

[a] 10 War Records, 471
[b] Roman's Military Operations of General Beauregard Extract from report of Lieutenant and Aid-de-camp A R Chisolm

road. On Monday, soon after daylight, he advanced along the Bark road with four regiments (Fifth, Twenty-third, and Twenty-fourth Tennessee, and the Fifteenth Arkansas), now reduced to 800 men, and became engaged in a thick underbrush at the left of General Breckinridge and the right of General Wood, where his brigade was repulsed and completely routed. The Fifteenth Arkansas was the only regiment rallied This continued in the fight until reduced to 58 men. These were then ordered to the rear to replenish ammunition

Shoup's batteries were in position Sunday morning on high ground south of Shiloh Branch Trigg's and Hubbard's batteries formed a part of Ruggles's line at 4 p m. Sunday. No information in regard to these batteries on Monday.

SECOND CORPS

(Bragg's)

This corps of two divisions formed the second line of battle and formed Saturday night, April 5, 1862 800 yards in rear of the first line across, and perpendicular to, the Pittsburg road; Gladden's brigade of Withers's division forward on Hardee's right; Ruggles's division on the left, its right on the Bark road; Withers's division to right of the Bark road The corps commenced its forward movement at about 6 30 a. m. on Sunday Soon after, the left brigade, Pond's, was detached to the left, and Chalmers's brigade moved forward to the right of Gladden The advance was continued in this order until Hardee's line became engaged, when Bragg, "finding the first line unequal to the work before it," moved his whole corps to its support. In this movement Ruggles's division intermingled with the first line, and the two corps were not again separated during the battle Withers on the right kept his Second and Third Brigades well in hand and leading them to the extreme right continued in command of them all day.

General Bragg in person followed his right and was with Gladden's brigade when Prentiss's camp was captured [a] There were present at that time General Johnston, General Bragg, General Hardee, General Withers, General Hindman, and several brigade commanders.[a] General Bragg remained in this vicinity until 10.30 a. m. when he met General Polk at the left center, and by agreement with him returned to the right center, where he directed several charges at Hornets' Nest without success. Learning that General Johnston had been killed, General Bragg went to the right and assumed command of the forces there, consisting of Breckinridge's two brigades, Withers's two brigades, and one brigade of Cheatham's division With this force he pressed the Union left along the Hamburg road until he reached the rear of Prentiss and Wallace and connected his troops with those of the extreme left This surround compelled the surrender of Prentiss about the time the sun was disappearing [b] Bragg re-formed his commands and was placing his troops in order for another advance when he received orders to withdraw his troops. Bragg remained with Beauregard near Shiloh Church Sunday night and Monday morning was sent to the Confederate left, where the troops of Pond, Wood, Cleburne, Cheatham, Gibson, Anderson, and Trabue were engaged, in

<hr>

[a] 10 War Records, 537, 567   [b] 10 War Records, 466

about the order named, from left to right Under General Beauregard's orders he commenced to retire his troops at 2 p. m.

In this division were the brigades of Gladden, Jackson, and Chalmers. It formed the right of Bragg's corps and formed in line Saturday night on the Bark road one-fourth mile east of the forks of Pittsburg Landing road. Gladden's brigade was sent forward to the first line, Jackson's brigade 300 yards directly in rear of Gladden, on right of Bark road, Chalmers's, on Jackson's right, extending the line to tributary of Lick Creek.

In the advance Chalmers soon came up to Gladden's right and joined it in an attack upon Prentiss's camp. After capture of Prentiss's camp Withers was ordered, with Chalmers and Jackson, down the Bark road to Lick Creek to attack the Union left. He succeeded in driving Stuart back and following him, pressing back the Union left, reaching the rear of Prentiss and Wallace, and receiving the surrender of part of these troops. He then moved to the right along the ridge south of Dill Branch and formed in line, then advanced into the valley of Dill Branch, from which place he made the last attack Sunday. He then withdrew, his division becoming disorganized. Chalmers's brigade and one regiment of Jackson's brigade bivouacked in Stuart's camp; Withers personally in Prentiss' camp. On Monday the division had commenced to retire from the field and had marched 1 mile when it was recalled and engaged on the right until 2 p m , when it retired to Mickeys.

First Brigade.

This brigade was attached temporarily to Hardee's corps and took position Saturday night, April 5, at the right of the first line of battle, its left on the Bark road, in the following order, from left to right. Twenty-sixth Alabama, Twenty-fifth Alabama, Twenty-second Alabama, Twenty-first Alabama, First Louisiana, and Robertson's battery in rear of infantry

The brigade advanced at 6.30 a. m. Sunday along the line of Bark and Eastern Corinth roads until it became engaged, at 8.30 a. m., in front of Prentiss's camps. The Twenty-second Alabama formed across the Eastern Corinth road. The Twenty-sixth, crowded out of position on the left by Shaver's brigade, took position on the right In this attack General Gladden was mortally wounded, and Colonel Adams assumed command and drove Prentiss back, and at 9 a. m. took possession of his camps and formed his brigade in a square at Prentiss's headquarters, where it remained inactive until about 2 o'clock. At 2.30 Colonel Adams was wounded and Colonel Deas took command, and soon after led the brigade, except the Twenty-sixth Alabama, to the right and reported to General Breckinridge and became engaged in the last attack upon Prentiss. Here the Twenty-first and Twenty-fifth Alabama became separated from the brigade, and Colonel Deas formed the First Louisiana and Twenty-second Alabama (224 men) on the left of Jackson's brigade and remained in line until ordered back

to camp for the night. The Twenty-sixth Alabama meantime made a charge across the west side of Peach Orchard, supported on left by Forrest's cavalry in the woods. On Monday 150 men of the Twenty-sixth Alabama joined Chalmers in two engagements, and then left the field. The Twenty-first Alabama was in Colonel Moore's command on Monday,[a] the First Louisiana and the Twenty-second Alabama with Ruggles on the left of the line, where they were engaged until reduced to 60 men.[b] Robertson's (Alabama) battery of 12-pounder Napoleons was first engaged on Eastern Corinth road in front of Prentiss's camp. After that, from a position in Prentiss's camp, it engaged the Union batteries in Peach Orchard and then reported to Ruggles, east of Review field On Monday it was with the Confederate right. The Twenty-fifth Alabama joined a Missouri regiment on Monday[c] (First Missouri, Bowen's brigade).

Second Brigade.

(Chalmers's.)

This brigade, called the "Mississippi Brigade," formed the right of Bragg's line, its right resting on swamps of Lick Creek in the following order from left to right Fifty-second Tennessee, Fifth Mississippi, Ninth Mississippi, Seventh Mississippi, Tenth Mississippi, with Gage's (Alabama) battery in the rear It advanced at 6 30 a. m. Sunday and soon joined Gladden's right and made a gradual left wheel until it struck the left of Prentiss's camp and by a charge of the Tenth Mississippi, followed by the Seventh and Ninth Mississippi, the Eighteenth Wisconsin was driven from its camp at 9 a m, the three regiments pursuing across the ravine and to the hill beyond, where they came under fire from Hurlbut's division in the Peach Orchard and were ordered by General Johnston back to the captured camp. From the Eighteenth Wisconsin camp the brigade was conducted "by right flank file right" across the ravine and to the Bark road and along that road until its right rested on Lick Creek, where it re-formed its battle line facing north and advanced across Locust Grove Branch against Stuart's camps. When this advance began Union skirmishers fired into the Fifty-second Tennessee, stampeding the regiment so that only two companies could be rallied These companies were attached to the Fifth Mississippi. As the infantry advanced Gage's battery, stationed on high ground south of the ravine, shelled Stuart's camp, compelling him to move to his left rear, forming his left behind an orchard. Chalmers moved upon this position and drove Stuart back 300 yards to a ridge, where he maintained himself until about 2 p m, when he retired, closely followed by Chalmers, who was supported on his right by Clanton's cavalry, moving down the banks of the Tennessee. Swinging to the left against the exposed Union left, Chalmers's left reached the Hamburg and Savannah road near the camp of the Twenty-eighth Illinois, where he assisted in the capture of the troops of Prentiss and Wallace that had faced to the rear and were attempting to make their way to the river. The Fourteenth Iowa, a captain and four men of the Twenty-eighth Illinois, and colonel of the Eighteenth Missouri surrendered to the Ninth Mississippi. The brigade then moved directly east of the ridge south of Dill Branch until its

a 10 War Records, 556   c 10 War Records, 544.
b 10 War Records, 539.   d Chalmers's report

right was near the river, it then advanced into the valley of Dill Branch Skirmishers of the Ninth Mississippi crossed the ravine and ascended to the brow of the bluff, where they came under fire of the artillery.   "The brigade struggled in vain to ascend the hill, which was very steep, making charge after charge without success, but continued to fight until night closed hostilities on both sides "[a] Gage's battery was put in position in rear of the brigade, but was soon disabled and was compelled to retire, leaving one gun in the ravine in front of its position. It was not again engaged. The brigade retired to Stuart's camps, where it bivouacked Sunday night On Monday it was joined by several detached regiments and was engaged on the Confederate right south of Peach Orchard until 2 p m., when it received orders to retire. There are no reports on file from regiments or battery.

Third Brigade.

(Jackson's)

This brigade formed on the right of the Bark road in the second line, 300 yards in the rear of Gladden's brigade, in the following order from left to right Seventeenth Alabama, Eighteenth Alabama, Nineteenth Alabama, Second Texas, Girardey's battery in rear of infantry. It advanced at 6 30 a m. Sunday, following Gladden's brigade, and came up with that brigade at Prentiss's headquarters, where General Johnston in person ordered the brigade to the left in conjunction with movements of Wood and Shaver. Before it had proceeded far, the order was changed, and Jackson was ordered to follow Chalmers to the right, where the brigade formed on the south side of a deep ravine. Girardey's battery engaged the enemy in Peach Orchard from Prentiss's camp and then followed its brigade and took position at Shake-a-rag Church The brigade advanced directly against the camps of the Fifty-fourth Ohio and Fifty-fifth Illinois, the right of the brigade joining Chalmers and passing through the farm houses at the left of the Fifty-fifth Illinois camp and engaging the Seventy-first Ohio, while the left of the brigade engaged McArthur's brigade in the ravine east of Peach Orchard. At about 1 30 p m. Bowen's brigade joined Jackson's left, and together they advanced, driving back the Union force and making the left wheel with Chalmers Jackson reached the camp of the Twenty-eighth Illinois, in Chalmers's rear, and was present when prisoners were captured. The Eighteenth Alabama was detached to guard them to the rear. The other three regiments followed Chalmers to the right and took position in the valley of Dill Branch, where skirmishers went forward to top of bluff, where they came in range of artillery and "could not be urged farther." Finding an advance impracticable, an order was given to withdraw In the darkness the brigade became separated, the Seventeenth Alabama returning to the camp of Saturday night, and was out of the fight on Monday. The Nineteenth Alabama and Second Texas bivouacked with Chalmers, and on Monday were with the Twenty-first Alabama, organized as a temporary brigade, and fought on Chalmers's left. In an advance across an open field this force received an unexpected fire, which broke its line and disorganized the command, the Nineteenth Alabama, under Colonel Wheeler, alone remaining on the field until a general retreat

---

[a] Chalmers's report.

was ordered, when it formed a rear guard and remained at Mickey's several days. General Jackson, with the battery, bivouacked Sunday night at Shiloh Church. The battery was engaged with Cleburne on Monday and lost one gun and had its other guns disabled so that the cannoneers were detailed to another battery. General Jackson, unable to find his brigade on Monday, was not engaged. He reported at Corinth, Miss., at 11.30 p m. Monday.

FIRST DIVISION.

(Ruggles's)

This division of three brigades formed the left of the second line of battle, its right, Gibson's brigade, on the Bark road; its left, Pond's brigade, extending to near Owl Creek; its center, Anderson's brigade, on Pittsburg road

Soon after the forward movement commenced, Sunday morning, two regiments from the left were detached to guard the left flank of the army, and Gibson's brigade was moved to the right to support Shaver's brigade. Anderson's and the right of Pond's brigade moved directly forward and became engaged in front of the first encampments of the enemy, where Anderson's and Cleburne's brigades commingled and were disorganized, a part of each following the Pittsburg road, under Ruggles's command, until they reached Duncan Field about 3 p. m., when General Ruggles gave his personal attention to massing the artillery in front of the Hornets' Nest. Here he collected ten batteries and two sections and placed them along the road on the west side of Duncan Field and under their concentrated fire ordered Anderson and others to attack. This artillery fire drove away all the artillery from the Union lines at Hornets' Nest.

On Monday Ruggles, with portions of his division, fought on the Confederate left until the troops were ordered to retire, when he took command of the second line of the rear guard.

First Brigade

(Gibson's)

This brigade bivouacked Saturday night, April 5, 1862, on the right of Ruggles's division, its right on the Bark road, in order of regiments, from left to right: Fourth Louisiana, Thirteenth Louisiana, First Arkansas, Nineteenth Louisiana. (The battery belonging to this brigade—Bain's—was detailed to remain at Corinth. Yet it is enumerated in organization and referred to[a]—"we had our artillery at hand"—in such way that it may have been present.) The brigade followed Shaver's to the front of the first encampment, where, with its right in the woods and its left in the Rhea Field, it came under the fire of Waterhouse's battery, which was "on an eminence to the left and in the rear of the first line of camps" Passing through Peabody's camp it came up with Shaver's brigade and fired a few shots from the edge of Barnes Field at retreating Union troops and received a few shells from Munch's battery in reply. The brigade rested in Barnes Field until noon, when General Bragg found it "in rear of its proper place" and ordered it forward to an attack upon Tuttle and Prentiss

[a] 10 War Records, 382, 394, 486

at Hornets' Nest. The right of the brigade, the Nineteenth Louisiana, moved half a mile to the right across the Hamburg road and into a little farm (wheat field) and attacked the enemy in a dense undergrowth. The left of the brigade, the Fourth Louisiana, came into Duncan Field. The brigade was repulsed, but under Bragg's orders charged again and again, until they had been four times beaten back. After the fourth repulse the brigade retired to Barnes Field and was not engaged again on Sunday. The Nineteenth Louisiana, becoming separated from its brigade, bivouacked near Shiloh Church and on Monday joined the command of Marshall Smith on the right. The other regiments were on the left on Monday, next to Pond's brigade, where they charged the enemy and captured a part of a battery, but were unable to hold it. Pond was ordered to the right and Gibson held the extreme left[a] until ordered to retire.

Second Brigade.

(Anderson's.)

This brigade occupied the center of Ruggles's division in the second line Saturday night, April 5, its right on the Pittsburg road, "in column doubled at half distance on the center," but with room to deploy, its order from left to right: Twentieth Louisiana, Ninth Texas, First Florida Battalion, Confederate Guards' Response Battalion, Seventeenth Louisiana, Hodgson's Washington Artillery in rear. In the advance on Sunday the brigade was deployed and followed Cleburne's brigade and came up with it at 8.30 a. m. at the crossing of Shiloh Branch. It must have occupied the same ground charged over by Cleburne, for, the Twentieth Louisiana—on the left of Anderson's brigade—connected with Pond's right when the Second Tennessee—the left of Cleburne's brigade—retired through the Twentieth Louisiana,[b] and the right of Anderson's brigade—the Seventeenth Louisiana—joined the Sixth Mississippi—Cleburne's right—and the Eleventh Louisiana, of Russell's brigade, in a charge into the camp of the Fifty-third Ohio and were repulsed by the fire of Waterhouse's battery and its infantry support. The Seventeenth Louisiana, of this brigade, made three separate charges upon the Fifty-third Ohio camp. In the second and third charges the left wing of the regiment passed to the left of the Rhea House around the point of the ridge. The Confederate Response and Florida battalions attempted—in conjunction with the Eleventh Louisiana, of Russell's brigade—to cross the ridge, but were repulsed. This position was finally carried by the combined attacks of the right regiments of the brigades of Cleburne, Anderson, and Johnson, and the left regiments of Russell's brigade. During the struggle the Washington Artillery, together with artillery of the other brigades, occupied the high ground in the rear and rendered valuable aid in the attack. The Twentieth Louisiana and Ninth Texas, on the left, were twice repulsed, but with reenforcements carried the position held by Buckland's brigade and joined the right regiments in an advance upon McClernand's second position at the crossroads, where the brigade was partially reorganized and was engaged in front of Marsh's brigade camp. About noon it joined Trabue in his engagement with McDowell's brigade. At 3 p. m. this brigade moved

---

[a]10 War Records, 473.   [b]10 War Records, 471, 496, 497, 507, 585.

directly east along the Pittsburg road to Duncan Field, where the battery was placed in Ruggles's artillery line and the infantry moved to the right, where it joined other troops in an attack at the Hornets' Nest, where it was repulsed, and the Twentieth Louisiana retired from the field. The other regiments returned to the attack and followed the retiring Union troops to the place of surrender. The brigade then moved forward to a ravine—head of Dill Branch—where it remained fifteen minutes under artillery fire, and then, at sunset, retired, General Anderson, with the Ninth Texas and First Florida, bivouacking in the apple orchard, near the big spring. The other regiments were scattered, but were all represented with the brigade on Monday, and were engaged north of the Pittsburg road and later in front of Marsh's brigade camp. The Washington Artillery was engaged on Monday on the right, near the wheat field, where it lost three guns. The guns were recaptured, but it left three caissons and battery wagon and forge on the field.

Third Brigade

(Pond's)

This brigade formed the left of Bragg's line of battle Saturday night, its left near Owl Creek and extending beyond Hardee's left in the following order from left to right: Thirty-eighth Tennessee, Crescent Regiment, Eighteenth Louisiana, Orleans Guard, Sixteenth Louisiana, with Ketchum's Alabama battery in rear. At 8 a. m. Sunday the Thirty-eighth Tennessee, the Crescent Regiment, and one section of the battery were sent 1½ miles to the left to Owl Creek road. The other regiments and two sections of the battery, connecting with the left of Anderson's brigade, advanced to Shiloh Branch, where they became engaged with the skirmishers of McDowell's brigade. McDowell was ordered to withdraw and Pond gained the first line of camps without a conflict. Changing direction to the right, Pond was fired into by the Confederates and retired 100 yards and rested until about noon when he joined the left of Trabue's brigade in Crescent Field. He then moved forward to the valley of Tilghman Creek, where at 4.30 p. m. he was ordered by General Hardee to charge the Union lines, which were in position in the camps of the Fourteenth and Fifteenth Illinois He formed his regiments en échelon, the Eighteenth Louisiana in front on the left, followed by the Orleans Guard, and that by the Sixteenth Louisiana, and moved directly upon the Union line. He was repulsed with heavy loss and retired to high land on the west side of the creek, where he bivouacked Sunday night, with his right at Oglesby's headquarters, his left at Owl Creek

The Thirty-eighth Tennessee, the Crescent Regiment, and a section of Ketchum's battery, when detached in the morning, moved down Owl Creek road to the bridge on Purdy road, where they remained on guard until 2 p. m. when they were ordered to the center. They moved by the flank to cross-roads, where Beauregard ordered them to the east along Pittsburg road. At Duncan Field the section of artillery was placed on left of Ruggles's artillery line and the two regiments directed to the left, where they engaged the right flank of troops at the Hornets' Nest, Colonel Looney leading his regiment, the Thirty-eighth Tennessee, into the camp of the Third Iowa in time to assist in the capture of the Twelfth Iowa, the Crescent Regiment capturing a part of

the Prentiss troops The Thirty-eighth Tennessee then joined its brigade at Oglesby's headquarters. The Crescent Regiment bivouacked in a "near-by camp."

On Monday the brigade, except the Crescent Regiment, was engaged upon the extreme left of the army, and opened the battle by an artillery duel between its battery and those of Lew. Wallace. The brigade was driven back gradually to the Purdy road, when it was sent to join Trabue's right. It soon returned to the left and then fell back to the church disorganized. Colonel Looney, with his own regiment and parts of five other regiments (numbers not known), made the last charge of the day, his command forming at the church under personal direction of General Beauregard and charging forward directly over the site of Sherman's headquarters to near the Purdy and Hamburg road, then retiring through the rear guard stationed south of Shiloh Branch. The Crescent Regiment was sent Monday morning to the right, where it joined the Nineteenth Louisiana and First Missouri in support of the Washington Artillery,[a] and then in conjunction with Colonel Wheeler covered the retreat from that part of the field and camped at night at Mickey's. Ketchum's battery was engaged with the brigade all day and lost two guns [b]

FIRST CORPS.

(Polk's)

This corps of two divisions of two brigades each formed Saturday night in column of brigades behind the second line, its center on the main Corinth road, the first division in front.

In the advance Sunday morning the head of this corps passed Beauregard's headquarters, at the fork of the Bark and Pittsburg roads, at 7.04 a. m. At the Seay Field Stewart's brigade was detached to the right; Russell's brigade was led directly to the front and became engaged under the personal direction of division and corps commanders.

General Clark, commanding the division, led in the charge upon the camp of the Fifty-third Ohio, and soon after passing that camp was wounded and left the field. General Stewart succeeded to the command, but did not bring the division under his immediate orders.

General Cheatham, commanding second division, sent his first brigade directly to the front, where it was engaged under Polk's orders. He then took personal direction of Stephens's brigade, conducting it first to the left, and then at 10 30 a m. to the right center, where he was engaged at Hornets' Nest until about noon when he moved to the right and joined General Breckenridge and was engaged at Peach Orchard, and on Monday near the extreme left of the line.

CAVALRY.

The First Mississippi Cavalry operated as a reserve to Cheatham's division. At about 5.30 p m on Sunday, just after the surrender of Prentiss, it charged upon and captured Ross's battery as it was making its way to the river. It afterwards crossed the head of Dill Branch and started with 30 or 40 men to charge another battery, but finding itself in presence of the infantry, retired and proceeded to the bank of the Tennessee River at Brown's Ferry.

---

a 10 War Records. 524,   b 10 War Records, 543

Brewer's Cavalry.

Two companies were sent Sunday morning in the direction of Adamsville to watch the movements of Lew Wallace; other companies engaged in the rear of Russell's brigade until afternoon, when they were sent to the extreme left and were engaged against the Fourteenth Missouri and in Wharton's charge They bivouacked Sunday night in the valley of Tilghman Creek near Owl Creek

General Polk in person followed the line of the Pittsburg road. He assumed personal direction of the battle in front of Rhea House, directing the two brigades of his own corps and one each of Hardee's and Bragg's corps, and when the line was finally carried he pushed his commands forward without waiting to reorganize them. He says his three brigades—Stewart's, Russell's, and Johnson's— with occasionally a regiment from some other corps, fought over the same ground three times. He was present at the surrender of Prentiss and directed some of the troops toward the Landing, and when ordered to withdraw retired to his bivouac of Saturday night. On Monday he commanded the left center again and fought over the same ground as on Sunday. This corps and its divisions were entirely disintegrated before reaching the first camps of the enemy and did not again serve in the battle as divisions or corps.

FIRST DIVISION.

First Brigade

(Russell's)

This brigade bivouacked Saturday night across the Pittsburg road behind Stewart's brigade, in order from left to right, as follows: Eleventh Louisiana, Twenty-second Tennessee, Thirteenth Tennessee, Twelfth Tennessee, with Bankhead's (Tennessee) battery in the rear. In the advance on Sunday it followed the Pittsburg road to near Shiloh Branch, when it became engaged on the right of the road, its left, the Eleventh Louisiana, joining the Seventeenth Louisiana of Anderson's brigade[a] and the Sixth Mississippi of Cleburne's brigade in the attack upon the Fifty-third Ohio camp and the Union forces behind that camp. In this attack the Eleventh Louisiana was disorganized, a part of it afterwards joining Stewart's brigade[b] and a part continued under Russell for a time. The colonel and sixty men were engaged on the right on Monday.

The Twelfth Tennessee passed to the right of the Fifty-third Ohio camp into the Fourth Illinois Cavalry camp, where it joined Stewart's brigade, and supported the Fourth Tennessee in a charge upon McAllister's battery, and afterwards supported Bankhead's battery on the ground first occupied by McAllister. The Thirteenth Tennessee also passed to the right of the Fifty-third Ohio camp, then left wheeled and charged Waterhouse's battery in the flank, capturing two guns. It then moved directly past Shiloh Church, and from there along Pittsburg road to Duncan Field, where it supported Stanford's battery in Ruggles's artillery line. The Twenty-second Tennessee, remaining under Russell's command, moved through the camp and over the Waterhouse battery position to near the crossroads, where the Fifth Tennes-

---

[a] 10 War Records, 506, 511.   [b] 10 War Records, 428.

see, Lieutenant Colonel Venable, attached itself to Russell's command. Russell then joined Trabue's left in front of Marsh's brigade camp He then, with the Twenty-second Tennessee, moved into the valley of Tilghman Creek and up that creek to the place where Prentiss surrendered. Russell says that Prentiss surrendered to men of the Twenty-second Tennessee The Twelfth and Thirteenth joined Russell here, but no part of the brigade advanced beyond the place of surrender. The three regiments retired to Marsh's brigade camp and bivouacked Sunday night On Monday the remnant of the three regiments, a "very small force," was engaged on the left, next to Pond, for a time, and then fell back to Shiloh Church, where they came under the immediate command of General Beauregard, who bore the colors to the front, but was soon obliged to retire.

Bankhead's battery was engaged at the place occupied by McAllister's battery, and in Ruggles's line on Sunday, and on the right, Monday.

Second Brigade.

(Stewart's)

This brigade formed the advance of its corps and bivouacked across the main Pittsburg road in the following order from left to right: Fifth Tennessee, Thirty-third Tennessee, Thirteenth Arkansas, Fourth Tennessee, with Stanford's battery in the rear. It moved forward at 7 a. m Sunday morning one-half mile and deposited knapsacks, then passed the cotton press and its left regiment—the Fifth Tennessee—came into Fraley Field, where it received a shot from a Union battery that killed one man and cut the flagstaff. From "two cabins" General Johnston directed the brigade to the right, and conducted it toward the camp of the Eighteenth Wisconsin, where General Johnston went and met General Hardee [a] General Stewart moved his brigade by the right flank due east, from north side of Seay Field, until his right reached the Eastern Corinth road, his command in "open woods" in front of the enemy's (Peabody's) camp, "from which he had been driven." Here losing sight of General Johnston, he moved his brigade by left flank in line of battle through the camp and beyond it [b] Thence, cooperating with the left movement of Wood and Shaver. he moved "by the left flank," along the rear of Peabody's brigade camp, and behind Gibson's brigade, until the Thirteenth Arkansas was in the Fourth Illinois Cavalry camp, then by right flank in line of battle, and halted for orders Here occurred the "fire in the rear," occasioned by the Fourth Louisiana, on Gibson's left, firing to their left rear upon an officer "supposed to be a Federal." This left rear fire took effect in the ranks of the Thirteenth Arkansas. This regiment, mistaking the fire of the Fourth Louisiana for that of the enemy, returned the fire, and were joined by the Thirty-third Tennessee firing into the Twelfth Tennessee just then passing their front, and into the Eighth and Ninth Arkansas just being transferred to Wood's left.

From the Fourth Illinois Cavalry camp Stewart led his three left regiments north across a small stream and laid them down while he returned for the Fourth Tennessee, which he brought forward to the same place, but found that his three regiments had moved forward.

[a] 10 War Records, 404, 407. [b] 10 War Records, 433.

Here Stewart received orders to charge McAllister's battery at the northwest corner of Review field. He placed Stanford's battery in the Fourth Illinois Cavalry camp, and with the Fourth and Twelfth Tennessee behind it as a reserve, passed to the right behind Wood's brigade and joining Shaver's left charged the battery and captured one gun at 11 a. m., the Fourth and Twelfth Tennessee holding the ground where the battery had been stationed. Here General Hindman proposed to Stewart to join forces and attack the enemy on Shaver's right in Hornets' Nest. While arranging for this movement General Hindman was disabled and General Stewart took command of Hindman's force. Placing the Fourth Tennessee on the left of Shaver's brigade, he moved through the woods to Duncan Field and engaged the Union force that occupied the east side of that field until Shaver reported his troops out of ammunition, when Stewart withdrew the Fourth Tennessee to a position where it captured the gun and joined the Twelfth Tennessee, at about noon, in support of Bankhead's battery, which was being closely pressed by Union troops. The Fourth Tennessee then retired for ammunition.

In the meantime the Fifth and Thirty-third Tennessee and the Thirteenth Arkansas were by General Hardee's order moved forward from the ravine where Stewart left them and became engaged under Preston Smith's command near the crossroads. Later the Fifth Tennessee was attached to Russell's command farther to the left and then moved to the attack upon the right flank of the Hornets' Nest position. It then retired to a camp for the night. The Thirty-third Tennessee joined General Stewart again to the right of Ruggles's batteries and moved by the left flank along the road to the Forty-first Illinois camp, where it remained until night and then retired to a camp near the crossroads. The Thirteenth Arkansas, after its engagement at the crossroads, was in support of Smith's battery to the right, where Lieutenant Colonel Grayson was mortally wounded. It then retired to Beauregard's headquarters, and then to camp for the night near "Stewart's General Hospital."

The Fourth Tennessee, after its separation from General Stewart, joined Preston Smith's command in Marsh's brigade camp and was engaged from about 1 to 2 p. m. It bivouacked Sunday night near where it captured the gun.

General Stewart, after his own brigade had passed from his command, organized a command, consisting of Walker's Second Tennessee, part of the Eleventh Louisiana, and another regiment of Cleburne's command, and made a second attack at Duncan House. Falling back, he was joined by the Thirty-third Tennessee and moved along Pittsburg road and into the Hornets' Nest at the time of surrender. On Monday he had Bates's Second Tennessee and Thirteenth Arkansas under his command on the Confederate right. Colonel Strahl says the Fourth Tennessee was engaged on Monday "near the left of the line." He also says he was "on the left of the Washington Artillery." Washington Artillery was on the right Monday. The Fifth Tennessee was with Chalmers on the extreme right; Thirty-third Tennessee on the left with General Cheatham. Stanford's battery, after its first engagement Sunday in the camp of the Fourth Illinois Cavalry, became engaged on the right of Ruggles's artillery line and on Monday near the same place. It lost four guns.

SECOND DIVISION.

(Cheatham's)

This division of two brigades bivouacked Saturday night in the rear of the First Division, on the Pittsburg Landing road. Soon after the advance was begun on Sunday the Second Brigade was detached, under the command of General Cheatham, who directed its movements all day on Sunday. His personal movements are the same as the Second Brigade. Sunday night General Cheatham retired to his Saturday night bivouac. On Monday morning he was engaged for some time in arresting a stampede which came from the front. He then led the Sixth Tennessee, six companies of the Ninth Tennessee, the One hundred and fifty-fourth Tennessee, part of the Fifteenth Tennessee, and 100 men of Walker's Second Tennessee to an open field near Shiloh Church, where he received orders to report to General Breckinridge He moved half a mile to the right, then was ordered back and to the left. In this movement the One hundred and fifty-fourth Tennessee and Walker's Tennessee became detached and remained at the right. With parts of the One hundred and fifty-fourth, Ninth, and Fifteenth he moved northwest, passing near Shiloh Church; then to left of the Confederate line, where he was joined by Gibson's brigade and by the Twenty-seventh and Thirty-third Tennessee, and was engaged four hours. At 2.30 p. m. he was ordered to withdraw from the field

First Brigade.

(B. R. Johnson's)

This brigade moved forward Sunday morning along Pittsburg road with its division until 8.30 a. m., when it, in crossing Fraley Field, came under fire of the artillery. Here General Cheatham was detached with the Second Brigade, and Gen. B. R. Johnson led his brigade, first obliquely to the left, then by right flank until the center—left of Blythe's Mississippi—rested on the Pittsburg road, its regiments in order from left to right. Walker's Second Tennessee, Fifteenth Tennessee, Blythe's Mississippi, One hundred and fifty-fourth Tennessee, with Polk's Tennessee battery in the rear.

At the crossing of Shiloh Branch Johnson came up with the brigades of Cleburne, Anderson, and Russell, which had commingled and were making ineffectual attempts to force the Union lines General Polk at once assumed direction, and, without waiting to reorganize the shattered brigades, ordered the whole force forward without regard to corps, division, brigade, or even regimental organization. Blythe's Mississippi, with the Seventeenth Louisiana, moved around the point of the hill north of Rhea House and attacked Waterhouse's battery on its right flank In this action Colonel Blythe was killed, his regiment halting in a ravine between the battery and Shiloh Church. The One hundred and fifty-fourth Tennessee, with other troops, charged directly through the camp of the Fifty-third Ohio, and attacked Waterhouse's battery in front just as the Thirteenth Tennessee reached its left flank. Both regiments claim the two guns captured here. Polk awards them to the Thirteenth Tennessee. The One hundred and fifty-fourth pressed forward up the ridge toward Woolf Field, capturing another gun of Waterhouse's battery and one gun of

Schwartz's battery, near the crossroads. Here the One hundred and fifty-fourth was joined by the three left regiments of Stewart's brigades and took position in Woolf Field, where they were engaged for a time, and were then driven back.

General Johnson, who was engaged with his left regiments in the attack upon Barrett's battery and Buckland's brigade, after several repulses finally succeeded, in conjunction with other commands, in carrying the position, but was wounded in the final assault near the church at 11 a. m., he says, and the command passed to Col. Preston Smith, of the One hundred and fifty-fourth Tennessee. During this conflict Polk's battery was stationed near the Rhea House, where Captain Polk was severely wounded and his battery disabled, so that only one gun went forward to the crossroads, where it was captured. At the crossroads Colonel Smith learned of General Johnson's disability and took command of the brigade, which was now greatly reduced, the Fifteenth Tennessee having only 150 men, Blythe's Mississippi only 200. Smith formed his brigade "just beyond the crossroads, on the right of the broad avenue leading by the second encampment" (Marsh's). He had scarcely formed his line when the enemy advanced upon him through the woods from the north and made a fierce attack, which was kept up more than an hour, during which time Smith brought up the Fourth and Thirty-third Tennessee to reenforce his line He finally succeeded, at about 2 p. m., in driving back the enemy. He then moved along Pittsburg road to Duncan Field, where the One hundred and fifty-fourth Tennessee supported Swett's battery in Ruggles's line and the Second Tennessee (Walker's) supported the Thirty-eighth Tennessee. The Fifteenth Tennessee and Blythe's Mississippi were sent for ammunition and did not return None of this brigade advanced beyond the place of Prentiss's surrender. A part of the Second Tennessee bivouacked at the crossroads Blythe's regiment near Shiloh Church, the other regiments with Smith returned to Saturday night bivouac. On Monday the One hundred and fifty-fourth Tennessee, a portion of Blythe's Mississippi, and one company of Walker's Second Tennessee, under Colonel Smith, joined Chalmers on the Confederate right and retired with him in the afternoon. The Fifteenth Tennessee was engaged under Colonel Maney on the Confederate right.

Second Brigade

(Stephens's)

This brigade formed the rear of Polk's corps and bivouacked Saturday night across the Pittsburg road in the following order from left to right. Seventh Kentucky, Ninth Tennessee, Sixth Tennessee, First Tennessee (battalion) with Smith's (Mississippi) battery in the rear. Before the forward movement began on Sunday, Colonel Maney, with the First Tennessee (battalion) and the Nineteenth Tennessee from the Reserve Corps, was ordered to the right to guard a ford of Lick Creek. He did not return until 2.30 p m., when he rejoined his brigade at the Peach Orchard and assumed command of the same. In his absence Colonel Stephens commanded the brigade, which was accompanied by General Cheatham in person.

This brigade moved forward on the Pittsburg Landing road 1 mile when, at about 8.30 a. m., it was deployed to the left as a support to Bragg's line After half an hour it was ordered to the right, and at

10 a. m. reached a position in front of the Hornets' Nest where it formed with the right—Sixth Tennessee—in a little field (Wheat Field, see Walker's statement) and its left extended to Duncan Field.[a] Smith's battery was placed in position and engaged the enemy about an hour when the brigade made two assaults, its right in a thick underbrush, its left in an open field. It was repulsed, and its commander, Colonel Stephens, disabled. Falling back to the Hamburg road the brigade moved to the right at noon, and joined General Breckinridge's force south of the Peach Orchard.[b] Here Colonel Maney joined and assumed command of the brigade. At 2.30 p. m. he led the First, Ninth, and Nineteenth Tennessee in a charge across the Peach Orchard, in which he broke the Union line at the northeast corner of said field. The Sixth Tennessee and Seventh Kentucky were brought up by General Cheatham, and the brigade took position in a small ravine east of the Hamburg road and awaited a supply of ammunition. It was not further engaged on Sunday, the Nineteenth Tennessee returning to its own brigade, Statham's.

The First Tennessee and four companies of the Ninth Tennessee, under command of Colonel Maney, bivouacked Sunday night on the field, and on Monday were joined by the Fifteenth Tennessee and were engaged on the right of the Confederate line under General Withers. The Sixth Tennessee and six companies of the Ninth Tennessee retired Sunday night with General Cheatham to Saturday night's bivouac, and on Monday were engaged with him on the Confederate left until 2 30 p. m , when they were ordered to retire.

There is no record where the Seventh Kentucky camped Sunday night. On Monday it served under Breckinridge, near where some buildings were burned.

Smith's battery was first engaged for one hour in front of Hornets' Nest on Sunday. Two of its guns were engaged with General Cheatham on Monday.

The First Tennessee, under Colonel Maney, retired from the field at 4 p. m. on Monday and marched to Monterey and occupied the camp that it had been in before the battle. Colonel Maney claims that his battalion reached its camp "with but one single absentee not properly accounted for, and this one reached camp early next day."

RESERVE CORPS

(Breckinridge's)

This corps of three brigades bivouacked Saturday night along the Bark road, between Mickey's and the Pittsburg Landing road, in regular order of brigades, the First in advance and the Third in the rear.

At the intersection of the Bark and Pittsburg Landing roads the First Brigade was detached on Sunday morning and sent by main road directly to Shiloh Church. The Second and Third Brigades were led by General Breckinridge along the Bark and Eastern Corinth roads, and were put in position about noon by General Johnston in person, south of the Peach Orchard, where they were first engaged about 1 p m.

General Breckinridge served personally all day with his Second and Third Brigades, uniting them to his First Brigade at the time and

---

a10 War Records, 438   b10 War Records, 438, 537

place of Prentiss's surrender, and then conducted the entire command to the east along the ridge south of Dill Branch to near the river, where it was under fire from gunboats and batteries. At dark Breckinridge withdrew to encampments of the enemy.

On Monday he was engaged with his three brigades nearly intact on south side of Corinth road behind Duncan Field, his right joining Hardee about the Peach Orchard. When the army retired Breckinridge formed the rear guard

Morgan's squadron of Kentucky cavalry and Phil Thompson's company (Kentucky cavalry) were attached to this corps, but do not appear to have been engaged.

First Brigade.

(Trabue's)

This brigade formed the advance of the reserve corps and reached the forks of the Bark and Pittsburg roads about 8 a. m. Sunday morning, April 6, 1862. It was sent forward on Pittsburg road to support General Polk's line and soon after deployed to the left of the road in the following order from left to right Fourth Kentucky, Sixth Kentucky, Thirty-first Alabama, Fifth Kentucky, Fourth Alabama, Crew's Tennessee battalion, Third Kentucky, with Cobb's (Kentucky) battery and Byrne's (Mississippi) battery in the rear

It passed Shiloh Church in line of battle about 11.30 a. m.—the Fifth Kentucky opening to right and left to pass the Church (Lofland's statement). It advanced due north from the Church to the "verge of a large crescent-shaped field" Here the Third Kentucky, Fourth Alabama, and Crew's battalion and Byrne's battery were detached by General Beauregard and ordered to support General Anderson on the right. The Third and Fourth Kentucky remained detached all day, there is no record of place where they were engaged Cobb's battery was put in position in front of the Fifth Kentucky in the avenue in front of Marsh's brigade camp. Colonel Trabue sheltered his command in a slight ravine, on the verge of the field, and rode forward to make observations. He discovered two camps to his left and front (Hare's and Marsh's), the enemy still occupying the camps. He moved his command by the left flank into this field and confronted the enemy. Here he was joined on the left by parts of Russell's and Cleburne's brigades—Twenty-second Tennessee, part of Eleventh Louisiana, Fifth Tennessee (Venable), and Fifth Tennessee (Hill)—and on his right by part of Anderson's brigade. The Union troops mentioned by Trabue in his front were the Forty-sixth Ohio, Sixth Iowa, and Thirteenth Missouri. After an engagement of one hour and a quarter, commencing about noon, Trabue ordered a charge and drove the enemy through their camp (Marsh's) and into the woods in the rear, where he encountered and dispersed a Missouri regiment and soon after reached the field where Prentiss surrendered, where his left joined the troops from the right, and Crew's battalion was detached with prisoners In the meantime Cobb's battery, occupying its first position in Marsh's camp, had been taken and retaken. It had lost all of its horses and was abandoned. Four of its guns were removed with mules Sunday night, but the battery was not again in action. Byrne's battery was engaged in Ruggles's artillery line.

After the surrender of Prentiss, Trabue, with the Fourth, Fifth, and Sixth Kentucky and Thirty-first Alabama joined Breckinridge and moved down the ridge south of Dill Branch and occupied a position on the crest of the hill, at mounds, overlooking the Tennessee River, where he came under fire from gunboats, which he endured until nearly dark, when he withdrew to the crossroads, where he was joined by the Third Kentucky, Fourth Alabama, and Byrne's battery, and then retired to the camps of the Sixth Iowa and Forty-sixth Ohio, where he passed Sunday night Trabue says he rode until 11 o'clock, trying to find a general officer to whom he could report for orders, and then sent an aid with escort, who rode all night without success.

On Monday morning the brigade formed on the Purdy Road, Byrne's battery at Owl Creek Bridge. In a short time the brigade was moved by the flank to a point three-fourths of a mile east of Shiloh Church, and formed in line on the left and perpendicular to the road, Byrne's battery on the road at edge of a field (Duncan's), with Anderson[a] on the left and Bowen's brigade on the right This position was held four hours and then the brigade, except the Fourth Kentucky and Fourth Alabama, moved to the right of the Duncan House and was then engaged for one hour more, when it fell back to the right of Shiloh Church The Fourth Kentucky and Fourth Alabama were engaged in severe conflict north of Duncan Field, where they lost very heavily. Major Monroe, Fourth Kentucky, was killed here. At Shiloh Church the contest was continued two hours, when the brigade fell back to the forks of Bark and Pittsburg roads, where it remained as a rear guard Monday night, and on Tuesday retired to Mickey's, where it remained three days.

Second Brigade.

(Bowen's)

From its bivouac Saturday night on the road toward Mickey's this brigade marched by the Bark and Eastern Corinth roads Sunday morning to a position between the Peach Orchard and Locust Grove Creek, where it formed in battle line at 12[a] o'clock under the personal direction of General Johnston in the following order from left to right Ninth Arkansas, Tenth Arkansas, Second Confederate, First Missouri, with Hudson's (Mississippi) and Watson's (Louisiana) batteries in the rear, its left 800 yards to rear and en échelon to Jackson's brigade. From this position it moved forward at 12.30[b] p m. and became engaged, in conjunction with Jackson, in an attack upon McArthur's brigade just east of the Peach Orchard The attack was successful; the Union line was driven back and pursued to the northeast corner of the Peach Orchard. General Johnston, following close to the rear of this brigade, was killed at 2.30 p. m.

Bowen was next engaged at Wicker Field with troops at the camp of the Twenty-eighth Illinois for two hours, when he was wounded and his brigade fell back to Seventy-first Ohio camp, where Colonel Martin took command and moved forward in time to join Breckinridge in his movement toward the river after the surrender of Prentiss. Martin says he halted within 300 or 400 yards of the river when the

---

[a] 10 War Records, 618   [b] 10 War Records, 404

batteries near Pittsburg and the gunboats opened on him, and being nearly night he fell back "to the first encampment the farthest from the river" and stayed all night. On Monday he was engaged under Breckinridge and fell back with him to the Bark road, where he bivouacked Monday as rear guard.

No mention in the reports of either Hudson's or Watson's batteries.

Third Brigade

(Statham's)

This brigade formed the rear of the army and consisted of the Fifteenth and Twenty-second Mississippi. the Nineteenth, Twentieth, Twenty-eighth, and Forty-fifth Tennessee, and Rutledge's Tennessee battery.

It followed Bowen's brigade, and at noon was put in line south of Peach Orchard en échelon to and 800 yards in rear of Bowen. It moved forward into the Orchard, and at about 2 20 p m was put in position by Governor Harris and ordered to attack the Union forces at Bloody Pond. It moved to this attack in conjunction with Colonel Maney. After the surrender it joined Breckinridge in his movement east on the ridge It is not known where it bivouacked Sunday night On Monday it was doubtless engaged with Breckinridge, but there are no reports of brigades or regiments.

Rutledge's battery was first in action on a hill in the rear of the brigade, then reported to General Ruggles and formed a part of his artillery line. On Monday it was near Shiloh Church The Nineteenth Tennessee went with Colonel Maney Sunday to Lick Creek and was with him in the charge at Peach Orchard at 2.30 p m , and at the time of the surrender of Prentiss was with Colonel Looney, Thirty-eighth Tennessee, at the camp of the Third Iowa.

The Twentieth Tennessee must have been engaged Monday with Breckinridge—its colonel, Battle, was captured in the vicinity of Lost Field by the Seventy-seventh Pennsylvania.

UNATTACHED CAVALRY.

Forrest's (Tennessee) regiment was guarding the fords of Lick Creek until about 2.30 p m Sunday, when it arrived on the field and supported the left of the Twenty-sixth Alabama in the thick wood west of Peach Orchard.

Clanton's (Alabama) regiment moved down the Bark road to Lick Creek, and then down the banks of the Tennessee River, guarding the right flank of the army all day Sunday

Wharton's Texas Rangers was on the left and at about 4.30 p. m Sunday made a charge at Cavalry Field; was repulsed and Wharton wounded. It encamped on the left of the army and supported Ketchum's battery Monday, and in the afternoon charged the Union right and was repulsed.

Adams's (Mississippi) cavalry was at ford of Lick Creek until 2.30 p. m. Sunday, then in reserve.

"Louisiana Cavalry" is mentioned, not certain whether or not it was Scott's First Louisiana.

89

DESIGNATION OF BATTERIES MENTIONED HEREIN.

Austin. (*See* Trigg's Alabama)
Bain's Mississippi
Bankhead's Tennessee
Barrett's B, 1st Illinois.
Bartlett's G, 1st Ohio
Behr's 6th Indiana.
Bouton's I, 1st Illinois
Buel's. (*See* Thurber's 1st Missouri)
Burrows's 14th Ohio.
Byrne's Mississippi.
Cavender's (*See* D, H, and K, 1st Missouri)
Calvert's Arkansas
Cobb's Kentucky
Dresser's D, 2d Illinois
Gage's Alabama
Gibson's Field Battery
Girardey's Georgia
Harper's Mississippi
Helena. (*See* Calvert's Arkansas)
Hickenlooper's 5th Ohio
Hodgson's (*See* Washington, Louisiana No 5)
Hubbard's Arkansas
Hudson's Mississippi
Jefferson (*See* Harper's)
Ketchum's Alabama
Lyon's (*See* Cobb's Kentucky)
Mann's C, 1st Missouri
Markgraf's 8th Ohio
McAllister's D, 1st Illinois.
McClung's Tennessee
Mendenhall's H and M, 4th United States.
Meyer's 13th Ohio.

Miller's Tennessee
Morton (*See* Behr's 6th Indiana)
Munch's 1st Minnesota.
Pettus Flying Artillery (*See* Hudson's)
Pillow's Flying Artillery (*See* Miller's)
Polk's Tennessee.
Powell's F, 2d Illinois
Richardson's D, 1st Missouri.
Robert's Arkansas
Robertson's Alabama or Florida
Ross's 2d Michigan
Rutledge's Tennessee
Schwartz's E, 2d Illinois
Shoup's. (*See* Calvert's, Trigg's, and Hubbard's)
Silfversparre's H, 1st Illinois.
Smith's Mississippi
Stanford's Mississippi
Stone's K, 1st Missouri
Swett's Mississippi
Taylor's (*See* Barrett's 1st Illinois)
Terrill's H, 5th United States
Thompson's, 9th Indiana
Thurber's I, 1st Missouri
Timoney's (*See* Dresser's 2d Illinois)
Trigg's Arkansas
Vaiden's (*See* Bain's)
Warren Light Artillery (*See* Swett's)
Washington, Louisiana No 5
Washington, Georgia (*See* Girardey's)
Waterhouse's E, 1st Illinois
Watson's Louisiana
Welker's H, 1st Missouri
Willard's A, 1st Illinois
Wood's (*See* Willard's A, 1st Illinois)

Abstract of Field Returns "Present" and "Casualties" at Shiloh April 6-7, 1862.

ARMY OF THE TENNESSEE

Command	For duty Officers	For duty Men	For duty Total	Extra duty Officers	Extra duty Men	Sick Officers	Sick Men	In arrest Officers	In arrest Men	Total present	Number engaged as reported by commander	Killed	Wounded	Missing	Casualties Total	Batteries	Guns in action	Guns lost
MCLERNAND'S (FIRST) DIVISION (Returns of Mar 31 and Apr 8, 1862) Division staff																		
Hare's (First) Brigade																		
8th Illinois	28	465	493								476	30	91	3	124			
18th Illinois	23	367	390								400	17	68	2	87			
11th Iowa	35	631	666								750	33	160	1	194			
13th Iowa	38	632	665								717	20	139	3	162			
Total First Brigade (note *a*)	119	2,095	2,214	5	75	10	215	1	1	2,521	2,414	100	458	9	667	2		
Marsh's (Second) Brigade																		
11th Illinois	14	318	332								239	17	69	17	103			
20th Illinois	20	506	526									22	107	7	136			
45th Illinois	27	535	562									23	187	3	213			
48th Illinois	23	404	427									18	112	3	133			
Total Second Brigade (note *a*)	84	1,768	1,847	4	81	11	284	1		2,228	1,514	80	475	30	585			
Raith's (Third) Brigade																		
17th Illinois	19	577	596								400	15	118	5	138			
29th Illinois	28	559	587								500	12	73	4	89			
43d Illinois	36	586	622									50	118	29	197			
49th Illinois	26	522	548									19	83	8	110			
Total Third Brigade (note *a*)	109	2,044	2,153	3	118	8	273	1	10	2,685	1,050	96	392	46	534			

Organization	Officers present for duty	Men present for duty	Aggregate present	Aggregate present and absent
Artillery				
Dresser's battery (D), 2d Illinois	5	108	108	107
Schwartz's battery (E), 2d Illinois	3	75	78	81
McAllister's battery (D), 1st Illinois	2	60	62	77
Burrow's battery, 14th Ohio	3	100	118	130
Total artillery	13	343	366	496
Cavalry				
Carmichael's (Illinois) company	3	64	67	68
Stewart's (Illinois) company	3	54	57	68
1st Battalion, 4th Illinois	16	231	247	335
Total cavalry	22	349	371	471
Total First Division (note a)	347	6,694	6,941	8,270
W H L WALLACE'S (SECOND) DIVISION (Return of Apr 5)				
Division staff				
Tuttle's (First) Brigade				
2d Iowa	25	465	490	615
7th Iowa	18	385	383	537
12th Iowa	26	463	489	689
14th Iowa	21	421	442	511
Total First Brigade	90	1,714	1,804	2,382
McArthur's (Second) Brigade				
Brigade staff				
9th Illinois	24	593	617	757
12th Illinois	23	444	467	619
13th Missouri	26	512	538	679
14th Missouri	23	486	458	611
81st Ohio	22	445	468	500
Total Second Brigade	118	2,430	2,548	3,166
Sweeny's (Third) Brigade				
8th Iowa	31	658	689	772
7th Illinois	29	617	546	627
50th Illinois	29	501	590	647
52d Illinois	23	618	641	744
57th Illinois	35	678	613	754
58th Illinois	29	523	502	654
Total Third Brigade	176	3,395	3,571	4,198

Abstract of Field Returns "Present" and "Casualties" at Shiloh April 6-7, 1862—Continued.

ARMY OF THE TENNESSEE—Continued.

Command	For duty Officers	For duty Men	For duty Total	Extra duty Officers	Extra duty Men	Sick Officers	Sick Men	In arrest Officers	In arrest Men	Total present	Number engaged as reported by commander	Killed	Wounded	Missing	Total	Batteries	Guns in action	Guns lost
W. H. L. WALLACE'S (SECOND) DIVISION—cont'd. (Return of Apr. 5.)																		
Artillery.																		
Willard's battery (A), 1st Illinois	4	106	110				10			120		4	26		30	1	6	
Richardson's battery (D), 1st Missouri													6		6	1	4	
Welker's battery (H), 1st Missouri	8	173	181	2	13		15			211			17		17	1	4	
Stone's battery (K), 1st Missouri															4	1		
Total artillery	12	229	291	2	13	43	25			331		4	53		57	4	18	18
Cavalry.																		
Companies A and B 2d Illinois	4	122	126		5		17			148		1	5		6			
Company C, 2d, and Company I, 4th United States	1	67	68		10		8			86								
Total cavalry	5	189	194		15		25			234		1	5		6			
Total Second Division	401	8,007	8,408	16	600	43	1,214			10,281		270	1,173	1,306	2,749	4	18	
LEW. WALLACE'S (THIRD) DIVISION. (Return of Apr. 4.)																		
Smith's (First) Brigade.																		
11th Indiana	21	610	631	1	24	1	96			733		11	51		62			
24th Indiana	29	665	694	1	18	1	21			735		6	45		51			
8th Missouri	15	658	673	3	56	4	53			789		1	18		19			
Total First Brigade	65	1,933	1,998	5	98	6	170			2,277		18	114		182			

Thayer's (Second) Brigade.

1st Nebraska	21	525	549		61	6	77	695	4	22	2	28	
23d Indiana	21	612	633			9	71	713	7	35	1	43	5
58th Ohio	29	601	630		21	5	80	736	9	42		51	6
68th Ohio *	29	395	424	2	49	6	167	646					
Total Second Brigade	103	2,133	2,236	2	131	26	395	2,790	20	99	3	122	11

Whittlesey's (Third) Brigade.

20th Ohio	25	466	491		28		56	900	1	19		20	1
56th Ohio *	32	669	701	1	11	2	48	762			1		1
76th Ohio	26	638	714		19	4	96	884	1	4		5	
78th Ohio	28	607	685		3	3	47	688	1	9	1	10	
Total Third Brigade	111	2,430	2,541	1	56	9	277	2,884	2	32	1	35	2

Artillery.

Buel's battery (1), 1st Missouri	2	116	118				1	122	1	1	1	1	1
Thompson's battery, 9th Indiana	5	107	112		3		10	122		5		6	1
Total artillery	7	223	230		3		11	244	1	6		7	2

Cavalry.

3d Battalion, 11th Illinois *	14	262	276		6		12	294					
3d Battalion, 5th Ohio *	14	269	283		7		38	328					
Total cavalry	28	531	559		18		50	622					
Total Third Division	314	7,250	*7,564	8	301	41	903	8,817	41	251	4	296	11

HURLBUT'S (FOURTH) DIVISION.
(Return of Apr. 5.)

Williams's (First) Brigade.

3d Iowa	27	589	560	1	24	8	182	776	53	131	20	187	
28th Illinois	27	615	642		11	3	76	782	29	211	5	245	
32d Illinois	25	627	652	1	21	2	96	777 558	39	114	5	158	
41st Illinois	23	600	568	1	18	2	60	634	21	73	3	97	
Total First Brigade	96	2,311	2,407	3	74	20	414	2,918	112	532	43	687	

* 2 regiments of infantry, 2 battalions of cavalry, 1 gun of Buel's battery, and train guard—a total of 1,727—were left at Crimps Landing, making the number actually engaged at Shiloh 5,887. Wallace says 5,000.

Abstract of Field Returns "Present" and "Casualties" at Shiloh, April 6–7, 1862—Continued.

ARMY OF THE TENNESSEE—Continued.

Command.	For duty. Officers.	For duty. Men.	For duty. Total.	Extra duty. Officers.	Extra duty. Men.	Sick. Officers.	Sick. Men.	In arrest. Officers.	In arrest. Men.	Total present.	Number engaged as reported by commander.	Killed.	Wounded.	Missing.	Total.	Batteries.	Guns in action.	Guns lost.
HURLBUT'S (FOURTH) DIVISION—Continued. (Return of Apr. 5.)																		
Veatch's (Second) Brigade.																		
14th Illinois	30	692	722	1	21		57			802		35	126	4	165			
15th Illinois	22	617	639	4	31	1	57			731		49	117		166			
46th Illinois	29	681	710	4	27	1	98			837		25	134	1	160			
25th Indiana	29	622	651	1	6		92			760		21	115	3	139			
Total Second Brigade	110	2,612	2,722	6	86	2	304			3,120	600	130	492	8	630			
Lauman's (Third) Brigade.																		
31st Indiana	19	375	594	2	24	5	104			729	478	21	114	3	138			
44th Indiana	22	506	528	1	41	4	94			668		24	174	1	198			
17th Kentucky	20	354	374	1	25	5	168			673	250	18	69		88			
25th Kentucky	16	239	255		26		117			398	200	7	27		34			
Total Third Brigade	77	1,674	1,751	4	116	14	483			2,868	1,727	70	384	4	458			
Artillery.																		
Ross's battery, 2d Michigan	4	90	84		4		6			90			5	36	61	1	6	
Mann's battery (C), 1st Missouri	3	89	89	1			5			99		3	14		17	1	4	5
Meyer's battery, 13th Ohio	4	78	80				10			90		1	8		9	1	6	6
Total artillery	11	242	258	1	4		21			279		4	27	56	87	3	16	11
Cavalry.																		
1st and 2d Battalions, 5th Ohio	35	657	692		8	1	66			757		1	6		7			
Total Fourth Division	329	7,496	7,825	14	288	37	1,278			9,442		317	1,441	111	1,869	3	16	11

SHERMAN'S (FIFTH) DIVISION
(Return of Apr 5)

	Present for duty officers	Present for duty men	Aggregate present								Aggregate present and absent		Pieces of artillery	Horses		Aggregate			
Division staff	..	..	..	.	..	......	..	..	..	...	....	..	1	..	1	...	..	....
McDowell's (First) Brigade																		
6th Iowa	27	605	632	1	68	3	34		738	..	.	52	94	37	183	...	..	....
46th Ohio	25	676	701	..	48	11	115		875	.	.	37	185	24	246	...		..
40th Illinois	20	577	597	1	28	11	108		745	.	.	47	160	9	216			..
Total First Brigade	72	1,858	1,930	2	144	25	257		2,358		.	136	439	70	645		....	.
Stuart's (Second) Brigade																		
55th Illinois	29	628	657	5	90	4	31	..	787			51	197	27	275	..	......	....
54th Ohio	29	586	615	3	8	5	97	..	..	728	..	15	139	12	166	...	..	....
71st Ohio	27	640	667	..	47	7	99	..	820		510	14	44	51	109		..	...
Total Second Brigade	85	1,854	1,939	8	145	16	227	..	2,835	..	.	80	380	90	550		-	...
Hildebrand's (Third) Brigade																		
53d Ohio	27	619	646	..	13	10	206	..	875	..	.	9	33	2	44	..	. .	...
57th Ohio	24	518	542	..	50	11	201	..	804	..	.	10	72	12	94	..	....	....
77th Ohio	26	619	645		15	7	121	..	788	..	.	51	116	51	218	..	....	....
Total Third Brigade	77	1,756	1,833		78	28	528	..	2,467	..	..	70	221	65	356	..	...	.
Buckland's (Fourth) Brigade																		
48th Ohio	33	573	606	3	25		128	..	762	..		12	78	18	103	..	...	....
70th Ohio	35	819	854	2	4	..	51	..	....	907	...	9	57	11	77	.	..	....
72d Ohio	30	617	647	6	.. ..	1	178	..	836	..		15	73	45	133			....
Total Fourth Brigade	98	2,009	2,107	11	29	1	357	..	2,505	..	...	36	208	74	313	...		....
Artillery																		
Morton battery, 6th Indiana	5	110	115	...	7		8		130	..	.	1	5	...	6	1	6	5
Taylor's battery (B), 1st Illinois	4	108	112	...	..	..	8		120	...	.	1	5	..	6	1	6	..
Waterhouse's battery (E), 1st Illinois	3	100	103	...	... .		10	.	*113	...	.	1	17	..	18	1	6	3
Total artillery	12	318	330	...	7		26	.	363	..	.	3	27	.	30	3	18	8
Cavalry																		
2d and 3d Battalions 4th Illinois	16	275	291	......	29	4	49	..	373	..		..	6		6			....
Thielemann's Illinois (2 companies)	7	143	150	..	... .		6		156	..		. ..	..	..	.		.	....
Total cavalry	23	418	441	...	29	4	55	.	529	..	.	.	6	.	6			....
Total Fifth Division	367	8,213	8,580	21	432	74	1,450	.	..	10,567	...	325	1,277	299	1,901	3	18	8

*Estimated, no reports for March or April

Abstract of Field Returns "Present" and "Casualties" at Shiloh April 6-7, 1862—Continued.

ARMY OF THE TENNESSEE—Continued.

Command	For duty Officers	For duty Men	For duty Total	Extra duty Officers	Extra duty Men	Sick Officers	Sick Men	In arrest Officers	In arrest Men	Total present	Number engaged as reported by commander	Killed	Wounded	Missing	Total	Batteries	Guns in action	Guns lost
PRENTISS'S (SIXTH) DIVISION.																		
Division staff (Return of Apr. 5.)																		
Peabody's (First) Brigade.																		
12th Michigan	34	798	832	1	18		50			896		27	54	109	190			
21st Missouri	32	585	617	2	64		185			859		18	46	64	128			
25th Missouri	25	489	514	4	59	2	145			724		28	84	37	149			
16th Wisconsin	28	799	827	1	15	9	145			997		40	188	26	254			
Total First Brigade	119	2,671	2,790	8	171	12	525			3,506		113	372	236	721			
Miller's (Second) Brigade.																		
61st Illinois	21	416	437	4	5		255			701		12	45	18	75			
18th Missouri	28	524	552	1	49	3	136			741		15	82	147	244			
16th Iowa (note b)	36	749	785	1	14		59			859		17	101	13	131			
18th Wisconsin* (note d)	35	700	735				100			835		23	83	174	280			
Total Second Brigade	120	2,389	2,509	6	68	3	550			3,136		67	311	352	730			
Not Brigaded.																		
15th Iowa* (note c)	32	750	782				60			842		21	156	8	185			
23d Missouri* (note e)	35	640	675				60			645		27	59	410	496			
Total unbrigaded	67	1,290	1,357				120			1,477		48	215	418	681			
Artillery.																		
Hickenlooper's battery, 5th Ohio	4	133	137		9		10			147		1	19		20	1	6	
Munch's battery, 1st Minnesota	5	121	126				7			142		3	8		11	1	6	2
Total artillery	9	254	263		9		17			289		4	27		31	2	12	2

Cavalry															:	...	2
1st and 2d Battalions, 11th Illinois	3!	594	626	14	7	15	52		685		3	3	928	1,008	6	...	...	2
Total Sixth Division...	347	7,198	7,545		265		1,264		9,093		236	928	1,008	2,172	2	12	2
UNASSIGNED (note f)																	
Infantry																	
14th Wisconsin* (note g)	30	720	750				50		800		23	74	5	112	1	6	
15th Michigan* (note h)	30	720	750				50		800		16	74	3	93	1	4	
Total unassigned infantry	60	1,440	1,500				100		1,600		39	148	8	195	2		
Artillery																	
Markgraf's battery, 8th Ohio*	4	106	112				10		122			3		8	1	6	
Silversparre's battery (H), 1st Illinois*	3	80	83				8		91			2	6	6	1	4	
Bouton's battery (I), 1st Illinois*	4	108	112				10		122					2	1	6	
Siege guns (B), 2d Illinois*	4	108	112				10		122			6	3		1	6	
Powell's battery (F), 2d Illinois*	4	108	112				10		122			6	3	9	1	6	
Total unassigned artillery	19	512	531				48		579		39	11	9	20	5	2N	
Total unassigned	79	1,952	2,031				148		2,179		39	159	17	215	6	28	

* Estimated

Abstract of Field Returns "Present" and "Casualties" at Shiloh April 6–7, 1862—Continued.

ARMY OF THE TENNESSEE—Continued.

RECAPITULATION.

Command	Present: For duty Officers	For duty Men	For duty Total	Extra duty Officers	Extra duty Men	Sick Officers	Sick Men	In arrest Officers	In arrest Men	Total present	Number engaged as reported by commander	Casualties: Killed	Wounded	Missing	Total	Artillery: Batteries	Guns in action	Guns lost
First Division	347	6,594	6,941	12	274	34	996	2	11	8,220	7,028	285	1,372	85	1,742	4	20	13
Second Division	401	8,097	8,498	16	640	43	1,214			10,281		270	1,173	1,306	2,749	4	18	
Third Division	314	7,250	7,564	8	301	41	903			8,817		41	251	4	296	2	11	11
Fourth Division	329	7,496	7,825	14	288	37	1,278			9,442		317	1,441	111	1,869	3	16	11
Fifth Division	367	8,213	8,580	21	432	74	1,450			10,557		395	1,277	299	1,901	3	18	8
Sixth Division	347	7,198	7,545	14	265	15	1,264			9,053		236	928	1,008	2,172	2	12	2
Unassigned	79	1,962	2,031				148			2,179		39	159	17	215	5	28	
Total Army of the Tennessee	2,184	46,710	48,894	85	2,150	244	7,253	2	11	58,639		1,613	6,601	2,880	10,944	23	128	34
Infantry	1,956	41,801	43,757	82	2,042	294	6,643	2	11	52,771		1,483	6,385	2,705	10,633			
Artillery (note i)	83	2,171	2,254	3	36	4	273			2,570		25	193	65	283	23	128	34
Cavalry	145	2,738	2,883		72	6	337			3,298		5	23		28			
Total Army of the Tennessee	2,184	46,710	48,894	85	2,150	214	7,263	2	11	58,639		1,513	6,601	2,880	10,944	23	128	34
Deduct Third Division and unassigned infantry not on the field Apr. 6	374	8,690	9,064	8	301	41	1,003			10,417		40	399	12	451	2	11	
Aggregate, Army of the Tennessee, present at Shiloh Apr. 6 (note p)	1,810	38,020	39,830	77	1,849	203	6,250	2	11	48,222		1,473	6,202	2,818	10,493	21	112	34
Officers and men present for duty Apr. 6 (A. of T.) Reinforced Apr. 7 by the Third Division (see			39,830													21	112	
And by unassigned infantry			5,837													2	11	
			1,500															
Total			47,167													23	123	
Deduct losses			10,493															
Army of the Tennessee present Apr. 7			36,674													19	69	

Abstract of Field Returns "Present" and "Casualties" at Shiloh April 6–7, 1862—Continued.

ARMY OF THE OHIO.

(See note ‡.)

Command	For duty: Officers	For duty: Men	For duty: Total	Extra duty: Officers	Extra duty: Men	Sick: Officers	Sick: Men	In arrest: Officers	In arrest: Men	Total present	Number engaged as reported by commander	Killed	Wounded	Missing	Total	Batteries	Guns in action	Guns lost
M'COOK'S (SECOND) DIVISION. (Return of Apr. 30.)																		
Rousseau's (Fourth) Brigade.																		
6th Indiana	25	635	660			6	67			733		4	36	2	42			
5th Kentucky	24	701	726			3	56			784		7	56		63			
1st Ohio	22	686	708			3	47			757		2	47	1	50			
1st Battalion, 15th U. S. Infantry	17	501	518			2	27			561	336	4	59		63			
1st Battalion, 16th U. S. Infantry	16	374	390			1	56			447		6	50		56			
1st Battalion, 19th U. S. Infantry	10	196	206				33			529	294	5	32		37			
Total Fourth Brigade	114	3,093	3,207			18	286			3,511		28	280	3	311			
Kirk's (Fifth) Brigade.																		
34th Illinois	29	697	726				19			749		15	112		127			
29th Indiana	27	697	724			4	45			771		4	76		80			
30th Indiana	29	738	767				45			812		12	115	2	129			
77th Pennsylvania	21	483	504			2	37		1	642		3	7		10			
Total Fifth Brigade	106	2,615	2,721			7	146			2,874		34	310	2	346			
Gibson's (Sixth) Brigade.																		
32d Indiana	21	788	812			6	35			853		10	86		96			
39th Indiana	29	747	779			2	28			804		2	34	2	38			
15th Ohio	29	720	749			1	19			769		7	66		73			
49th Ohio	26	711	737			1	6			744		6	34		40			
Total Sixth Brigade	108	2,966	3,074			10	86			3,170		25	220	2	247			

Abstract of Field Returns "Present" and "Casualties" at Shiloh April 6-7, 1862—Continued.

ARMY OF THE OHIO—Continued

(See note f)

Command	Present — For duty			Extra duty		Sick		In arrest		Total present	Number engaged as reported by commander	Casualties — Killed	Wounded	Missing	Total	Artillery — Batteries	Guns in action	Guns lost
	Officers	Men	Total	Officers	Men	Officers	Men	Officers	Men									
M'COOK'S (SECOND) DIVISION—continued (Return of Apr 30)																		
Artillery																		
Terrill's battery (H), 5th United States	4	112	116							130		1	13		14	1	6	
Total Second Division	382	8,786	9,118			85	582			9,685		88	823	7	918	1	6	
Number Second Division engaged at Shiloh Apr 7*											7,563	88	823	7	918	1	6	
NELSON'S (FOURTH) DIVISION (Returns of Mar 31)																		
Division staff													2		2			
Ammen's (Tenth) Brigade																		
36th Indiana	19	489	508	1	16		11			536	380	9	36		45			
6th Ohio	18	697	715	1	32		13	1	6	761	698	2	5	2	9			
24th Ohio	23	630	653		30	1	23			714	550	5	65	6	76			
Total Tenth Brigade	60	1,816	1,876	2	78	1	47	1	6	2,011	1,628	16	106	8	130			
Hazen's (Nineteenth) Brigade																		
9th Indiana	24	623	647		52	2	39	1	4	741	569	17	153		170			
6th Kentucky	29	607	636		24	4	53		4	721	484	10	93		103			
41st Ohio	23	455	478	3	45		45			570	371	21	111	1	133			
Total Nineteenth Brigade	76	1,685	1,761	3	121	6	137	1	8	2,027	1,424	48	357	1	406			

Bruce's (Twenty-second) Brigade															
1st Kentucky	26	575	601				22	1	1	671	622	11	53	4	71
2d Kentucky	29	733	762				12	1	1	794	663	15	59	1	75
20th Kentucky	22	513	535				80		15	666	401	8	23	5	32
Total Twenty-second Brigade	77	1,821	1,808	6	112	5	114	1	1	2,136	1,589	29	138	11	178
Total Fourth Division	213	5,322	5,635	10	311	12	298	3	15	6,184	4,541	93	603	20	716
Total Fourth Division present at Shiloh Apr 7†											4,541	93	603	20	716
CRITTENDEN'S (FIFTH) DIVISION (Returns of Mar 31)															
Boyle's (Eleventh) Brigade															
9th Kentucky	27	468	495				18			513		15	76	1	92
13th Kentucky	25	503	529		1		10			540		8	41	10	59
19th Ohio	28	667	695		1		27			723		4	44	7	56
59th Ohio	22	438	460		1		14			476		6	51		67
Total Eleventh Brigade	103	2,076	2,170		8		69			2,251		33	212	18	263
Smith's (Fourteenth) Brigade †															
13th Ohio	4											11	48	7	64
11th Kentucky	4											5	48	2	55
26th Kentucky												9	61	1	71
Total Fourteenth Brigade												25	167	10	192
Artillery															
Bartlett's battery (G), 1st Ohio	4	114	118				14			132		2	2		2
Mendenhall's battery (H and M), 4th United States	4	62	66				6			77		2	6		8
Total artillery	8	176	184				19			209			8		10
Total Fifth Division											3,825	60	377	28	465
Number Fifth Division engaged at Shiloh Apr 7*											3,825	60	377	28	465
WOOD'S (SIXTH) DIVISION															
Garfield's (Twentieth) Brigade ‖															
13th Michigan															
64th Ohio															
65th Ohio															
Total Twentieth Brigade															

*Approximated Note ‡
†General Nelson's report (10 War Records, 326)
†No reports for March or April
‖No report for March or April Not engaged at Shiloh

Abstract of Field Returns "Present" and "Casualties" at Shiloh April 6–7, 1862—Continued

ARMY OF THE OHIO—Continued

(See note j)

Command	Present — For duty			Extra-duty		Sick		In arrest		Total present	Number engaged as reported by commander	Casualties — Killed	Wounded	Missing	Total	Artillery — Batteries	Guns in action	Guns lost
	Officers	Men	Total	Officers	Men	Officers	Men	Officers	Men									
WOOD'S (SIXTH) DIVISION—continued																		
*Wagner's (Twenty-first) Brigade * *																		
15th Indiana																		
40th Indiana																		
57th Indiana																		
24th Kentucky																		
Twenty-first Brigade †											2,000		4		4			
Total of Sixth Division engaged											2,000		1		1			

RECAPITULATION

Command	Number engaged	Killed	Wounded	Missing	Total	Batteries	Guns in action	Guns lost
Second Division	7,562	83	823	7	918	1	6	
Fourth Division	4,541	93	563	20	716	2	10	
Fifth Division	8,825	60	377	28	465			
Sixth Division	2,000		4		4			
Total Army of the Ohio	17,918	241	1,807	55	2,103	3	16	
Infantry	17,618	238	1,786	55	2,079			
Artillery	300	3	21		24	3	16	
Army of the Ohio Apr 7	17,918	241	1,807	55	2,103	3	16	
Army of the Tennessee Apr 7§	36,674	1,513	6,601	2,880	10,944	19	89	
Total Union Army Apr 7	54,592	1,754	8,408	2,885	13,047	21	105	

*No report for March or April   †Arrived at Shiloh just before the battle ended   Estimated   ‡Casualties, Apr 6 and 7   §See last line of the Army of the Tennessee, p 98,

Abstract of Field Returns "Present" and "Casualties" at Shiloh April 6-7, 1862—Continued

ARMY OF THE MISSISSIPPI

(See notes k, l, m, and n.)

Command	Present — For duty — Officers	Present — For duty — Men	Present — For duty — Total	Present — Extra duty — Officers	Present — Extra duty — Men	Present — Sick — Officers	Present — Sick — Men	Present — In arrest — Officers	Present — In arrest — Men	Total present	Number engaged as reported by commander	Casualties — Killed	Casualties — Wounded	Casualties — Missing	Casualties — Total	Artillery — Batteries	Artillery — Guns in action	Artillery — Guns lost
POLK'S (FIRST) CORPS																		
(Returns Mar 31, Apr 1, 3)																		
CLARK'S (FIRST) DIVISION																		
Russell's (First) Brigade *																		
11th Louisiana											500							
12th Tennessee												23	184					
13th Tennessee																		
22d Tennessee																		
Bankhead's (Tennessee) battery											93	2	18		20	1	6	
Total First Brigade												97	512	3	609	1	6	
Stewart's (Second) Brigade																		
13th Arkansas											806	45	72		100			
4th Tennessee												36	183		219			
5th Tennessee												20	103					
33d Tennessee												4	14	17				
Stanford's (Mississippi) battery											181			2	140	1	6	4
Total Second Brigade												90	421	3	517	1	6	4
Total First Division (report of Apr 1)	318	4,670	4,988								6,036	190	963	3	1,126	2	12	4

* Forty seventh Tennessee came upon the field Monday

Abstract of Field Returns "Present" and "Casualties" at Shiloh April 6–7, 1862—Continued.

ARMY OF THE MISSISSIPPI—Continued.

(See notes k, l, m, and n.)

Command	Present For duty Officers	Men	Total	Extra duty Officers	Men	Sick Officers	Men	In arrest Officers	Men	Total present	Number engaged as reported by commander	Casualties Killed	Wounded	Missing	Total	Artillery Batteries	Guns in action	Guns lost
POLK'S (FIRST) CORPS—Continued.																		
(Returns Mar. 31, Apr. 1, 3.)																		
CHEATHAM'S (SECOND) DIVISION.																		
Johnson's (First) Brigade.																		
Blythe's Mississippi											650		95	163	11	199			
Walker's 2d Tennessee											102		4	18	2	24			
15th Tennessee																			
154th Tennessee																			
Polk's Tennessee battery																	1	6	2
Total First Brigade													120	607	13	740	1	6	2
Stephens's (Second) Brigade.																		
7th Kentucky																			
1st Tennessee																			
6th Tennessee																			
9th Tennessee																			
Smith's (Mississippi) battery											120		1	18		14	1	6	6
Total Second Brigade											200		75	413	3	491	1	6	6
Cavalry (note n.)																		
1st Mississippi													2	10	1				
Brewer's Alabama and Mississippi																			
Total cavalry	44	621	665								847								
Total Second Division (report of Apr. 1)	192	2,840	3,082								4,576								
Total First Army Corps (infantry and artillery, report Apr. 8, 1862)	581	8,823	9,404	18	568	48	1,377	5	41	11,451			385	1,983	19	2,387	4	24	6

105

BRAGG'S (SECOND) CORPS
RUGGLES'S (FIRST) DIVISION
Gibson's (First) Brigade

1st Arkansas											
4th Louisiana											
13th Louisiana											
19th Louisiana											
Bain's (Mississippi) battery								1	6		
Total First Brigade	575	97	163	22	209			1	6		

Anderson's (Second) Brigade

1st Florida Battalion	250										
17th Louisiana	336										
20th Louisiana	507										
9th Texas	225										
Confederate Guards Response Battalion	169										
Washington Artillery No 5	155	14	42	11	67			1	6		
Total Second Brigade	1,638	69	313	62	434			1	6		

Pond's (Third) Brigade

16th Louisiana	330	19	46	27	92						
18th Louisiana		13	80	118	211						
Crescent Louisiana		28	84	20	127						
Orleans Guard Battalion		17	65	18	90						
38th Tennessee		7	43	15	65						
Ketchum's (Alabama) battery		1	12	1	14					6	2
Total Third Brigade		89	336	169	694					6	2

Cavalry (note n)
Jenkin's (Alabama) Battalion * — 228 | 2 | 5 | 1 | 8 | | | | | | |

Total First Division (returns Mar 31) — 6,484 | 255 | 1,137 | 318 | 1,710 | 473 | 7,199 | 7,672 | 3 | 18 | | 2

WITHERS'S (SECOND) DIVISION
Gladden's (First) Brigade

21st Alabama											
22d Alabama	445				198						
25th Alabama	305										
26th Alabama	440										
1st Louisiana										4	
Robertson's (Alabama) battery								1		4	
Total First Brigade		129	597	108	829			1		4	

*Not included in division total

Abstract of Field Returns "Present" and "Casualties" at Shiloh April 6-7, 1862—Continued

ARMY OF THE MISSISSIPPI—Continued

(See notes k, l, m and n)

Command	Present									Total present	Number engaged as reported by commander	Casualties				Artillery		
	For duty			Extra duty		Sick		In arrest				Killed	Wounded	Missing	Total	Batteries	Guns in action	Guns lost
	Officers	Men	Total	Officers	Men	Officers	Men	Officers	Men									
BRAGG'S (SECOND) CORPS—Continued																		
WITHERS'S (SECOND) DIVISION—Continued																		
Chalmers's (Second) Brigade																		
5th Mississippi																		
7th Mississippi																		
9th Mississippi																		
10th Mississippi																		
52d Tennessee																		
Gage's (Alabama) battery											400						1	6	
Total Second Brigade											2,089		85	343	19	445	1	6	
Jackson's (Third) Brigade																		
17th Alabama																		
18th Alabama																		
19th Alabama																		
2d Texas																		
Girardey's (Georgia) battery											120		10	80	30	120	1	6	1
Total Third Brigade											2,208		86	364	194	644	1	6	1
Cavalry (note m)																		
Clanton's 1st Alabama	49	621	670							822	*610								
Total Second Division (Mar 31)	479	7,391	7,873				3,678	3	12	10,109	6,182	298	1,304	316	1,918	3	16	1
Total Second Corps (report artillery and infantry, Apr 5)	1,028	15,251	16,279	23	663	112				21,791		763	2,441	644	3,848	6	34	3

HARDEE'S (THIRD) CORPS

HINDMAN'S TEMPORARY DIVISION

Shaver's (First) Brigade

- 2d Arkansas
- 6th Arkansas
- 7th Arkansas
- 3d Confederate
- Swett's (Mississippi) battery
- Miller's (Tennessee) battery

Total First Brigade — 2,360 ... 3,095 ... 646 ... 28 ... 693 ... 12

Wood's (Third) Brigade

- 16th Alabama — 325
- 8th Arkansas — 305
- 9th Arkansas Battalion — 165
- 3d Mississippi Battalion — 800
- 27th Tennessee — 380
- 44th Tennessee — 270
- 55th Tennessee — 850
- Harper's (Mississippi) battery — 8, 27 / 49, 115 / 2, 48 / 59, 190 / 1, 4
- Georgia Dragoons

Total Third Brigade — 83 ... 2,508 ... 93

Cleburne's (Second) Brigade

- Bate's 2d Tennessee
- 15th Arkansas
- 6th Mississippi
- Hill's 5th Tennessee
- 23d Tennessee
- 24th Tennessee
- Shoup's battalion, Arkansas Artillery
- Trigg's, Calvert's, and Hubbard's batteries — 365 ... 61 ... 239 ... 300 ... 3, 18

Total Second Brigade — 2,789 ... 149 ... 404 ... 790 ... 141 ... 1,043 ... 18

Total Third Corps (report Mar 31) — 7,657 ... 3,638 ... 11,217 ... 1,936 ... 2,481 ... 34 1

Official report of First and Second Brigades (vol 10 p 398) — 4,747 / 2,011 ... 4,392 / 1,928 ... 6,112 / 2,021

Wood's brigade (p 591) — 855 / 83

Total (note 1) — 6,758 ... 6,320 ... 8,183 †8,789 ... 404 ... 1,936 ... 141 ... 2,481 ... 6 ... 34 1

*Not included in corps total

†Hardee's report (10 War Records, 567)

Abstract of Field Returns "Present" and "Casualties" at Shiloh April 6–7, 1862—Continued

ARMY OF THE MISSISSIPPI—Continued

(See notes k, l, m, and n)

Command	Present — For duty			Present — Extra duty		Present — Sick		Present — In arrest		Total present	Number engaged as reported by commander	Casualties — Killed	Casualties — Wounded	Casualties — Missing	Casualties — Total	Artillery — Batteries	Artillery — Guns in action	Artillery — Guns lost
	Officers	Men	Total	Officers	Men	Officers	Men	Officers	Men									
BRECKINRIDGE (RESERVE) CORPS																		
Trabue's (First) Brigade																		
4th Alabama Battalion															30			
31st Alabama															79			
3d Kentucky															174			
4th Kentucky															213			
5th Kentucky															184			
6th Kentucky													30	183	108			
Crew's (Tennessee) battalion															56			
Byrne's (Mississippi) battery											481				14	1	6	6
Cobb's (Kentucky) battery															37	1	6	6
Morgan's (Kentucky) cavalry																		
Total First Brigade			2,691							3,422	2,400	151	557	92	800	2	12	6
Bowen's (Second) Brigade																		
9th Arkansas												17	115		182			
10th Arkansas																		
2d Confederate																		
1st Missouri																		
Hudson's (Mississippi) battery																1	6	
Watson's (Louisiana) battery																1	6	
Thompson's company Kentucky cavalry *																		
Total Second Brigade			1,744							2,199		98	498	28	624	2	12	12

Statham's (Third) Brigade.

Organization														
15th Mississippi														
22d Mississippi														
19th Tennessee														
20th Tennessee														
28th Tennessee														
45th Tennessee														
Rutledge's (Tennessee) battery.														
Forrest's (1st) Tennessee cavalry‡	679							785					1	6
Total Third Brigade Mar 31	438	3,679	12	169	66	1,039	2		3,727	187	627	45	809	1	6
Total Reserve Corps Apr. 3.	6,713	7,211	8	187	13	712	1	2	8,511	386	1,682	165	2,238	5	30

UNASSIGNED.

Cavalry.

Organization														
Wharton's (Texas) cavalry‡ / Adams's (Mississippi) cavalry†	60	1,315							2,298	7	56	4	67	1	6

Artillery.

Organization														
McClung's (Tennessee) battery														
Roberts's (Arkansas) battery‡														
Trabue's (Kentucky) battery‡														

* Not included in corps total.   † Estimated (see note n).   ‡ Uncertain; no record of such batteries; possible that Roberts's Arkansas was one of Shoup's battalion.

Abstract of Field Returns "Present" and "Casualties" at Shiloh April 6-7, 1862—Continued.

ARMY OF THE MISSISSIPPI—Continued.

RECAPITULATION.

(See notes k, l, m, and n.)

Command	For duty — Officers	For duty — Men	For duty — Total	Extra duty — Officers	Extra duty — Men	Sick — Officers	Sick — Men	In arrest — Officers	In arrest — Men	Total present	Number engaged as reported by commander	Killed	Wounded	Missing	Total	Batteries	Guns in action	Guns lost
First Army Corps	581	8,823	9,404	18	558	48	1,377	5	41	11,451		385	1,958	19	2,357	4	24	6
Second Army Corps	1,028	15,251	16,279	23	624	142	3,678	8	42	20,791		353	2,441	624	3,628	6	34	3
Third Army Corps	438	6,320	6,758	10	462	42	849	5	7	8,133		404	1,935	141	2,481	5	34	1
Reserve Corps	498	6,713	7,211	12	169	66	1,039	2	12	8,511		386	1,682	165	2,233	7	36	6
Total infantry and artillery	2,545	37,107	39,652	63	1,813	298	6,943	13	102	48,886		1,728	8,012	969	10,699	22	128	16
Cavalry (note n)	201	4,115	4,816	8	187	13	844	1	2	5,371								
Total Apr. 6 (note o)	2,746	41,222	43,968	71	2,000	311	7,787	16	104	54,257								
Deduct losses			10,699															
Total			33,269															
Add 47th Tennessee			731															
Total Apr. 7			34,000															
Confederates for duty Apr. 6 (note o)			43,968													21	112	
Union Army for duty Apr. 6 (note p)			39,830													22	128	
Confederate excess			4,138													1	16	
Aggregate engaged Apr. 6, Union and Confederate			83,798													43	240	
Total Union Army Apr. 7			54,592															
Total Confederate Army Apr. 7			34,000															
Union excess Apr. 7			20,592															
Aggregate in the field, both days: Union			66,812	85	2,150	244	7,253	2	11	76,567		1,754	8,408	2,885	13,047	26	157	
Confederates			44,699	71	2,000	311	7,787	16	104	64,988		1,728	8,012	959	10,699	22	128	16
Grand total			111,511	156	4,150	555	15,040	18	115	131,545		3,482	16,420	3,844	23,746	48	285	

NOTES.

UNION FORCES

(a) The "for duty" in the First Division of the Army of the Tennessee is made up from field returns of April 3, which is the latest return on file giving regiments in detail The "extra duty," "sick," and "in arrest" are from consolidated brigade reports of March 31, 1862

(b) The Sixteenth Iowa arrived at Pittsburg Landing on the 5th of April, 1862, and was assigned to the Sixth Division The morning report was made and is included in the report of Second Brigade, Sixth Division, for April 5, 1862 The regiment was preparing, on Sunday morning, to move out to the position of Sixth Division, when General Grant ordered it to duty at the Landing and later to a position in McClernand's line, it was not engaged with its division

(c) The Fifteenth Iowa arrived at Pittsburg Landing Sunday morning, April 6, 1862, under orders to report to General Prentiss Upon disembarking from steamboat it was, by General Grant, ordered to duty at the Landing with the Sixteenth Iowa, and later to a position in McClernand's line It is not included in the Sixth Division returns of April 5

(d) The Eighteenth Wisconsin arrived on the field April 5, 1862 It is not included in the returns made by the Sixth Division April 5, but it joined the Second Brigade of that division and encamped on the left of the brigade Saturday evening and was engaged as left regiment of Prentiss's division on Sunday

(e) The Twenty-third Missouri arrived on the field Sunday morning, April 6, 1862, and reported to General Prentiss at the "Hornets' Nest" about 9 a m and fought with him the remainder of the day

(f) Unassigned troops were all present on the 6th or 7th, but had not been assigned to a command and had not been taken up on the returns

(g) The Fourteenth Wisconsin arrived from Savannah Sunday night, and on Monday fought with Smith's brigade, Army of the Ohio The number present is estimated from returns of the Department of the Mississippi, March 31, 1862

(h) The Fifteenth Michigan fought on Monday with the Fourth Brigade, Army of the Ohio

(i) Guns lost on Sunday by the Army of the Tennessee were Burrows's battery, 6, Ross's battery, 5, Waterhouse's battery, 3, Hickenlooper's battery, 2, Dresser's battery, 4, Schwartz's battery, 2, McAllister's battery, 1 Abandoned, Behr's battery, 5, Meyer's battery, 6 Total, 34

(j) The Army of the Ohio has very meager returns on file except as to the Fourth Division The Second, Fifth, and Sixth Divisions are estimated from returns of March 20, March 31, and April 30, 1862 Compared with the Fourth Division returns of same dates and with Nelson's report ("Present at Shiloh" vol 10, War Records, pp 325, 326) General Buell says, in letter on file "I do not know whether the information was available at the time of making my report, but I have had it in my mind that my strength was between 18,000 and 19,000" He further says ' I estimate McCook's present for duty at 7,552 " Only one brigade (Wagner's) of the Sixth Division was engaged General Garfield says that his brigade did not reach the field in time to become engaged Only Wagner's brigade, estimated at 2,000, is included in present for duty of the Sixth Division

CONFEDERATE FORCES

(k) The tabulated statement on page 398, volume 10, War Records, "Marched from Corinth April 3, 1862," appears to have been compiled from returns of March 31 and April 1, 1862, and was not actually made out April 8 (See part 2 of vol 10, War Records, pp 377, 378, 382)

(l) The Third Corps, Hardee's, in tabulated statement, page 398, volume 10, has aggregate present, infantry, 5,750 On page 382, part 2, volume 10, return of April 1, Hardee's Corps has aggregate present 5,750, showing that the two returns are identical Both returns are also alike in artillery In the return on page 382, part 2, a note says that Hardee's return is of only two brigades, Wood's brigade being omitted, but is found on page 377 of part 2, volume 10 If Wood's brigade is omitted from return of April 1 it is also omitted from return of "Marched from Corinth ' and accounts for the difference between said last return and Hardee's official report, page 567, volume 10, which gives "effective present at Shiloh, 6,789 ' He had, April 1, present for duty, 6,758 (Enlisted for duty, 6,920, extra duty, 462, in arrest, 7, effective total, 6,789)

(m) The term "effective" is not uniformly used in the Confederate reports In returns "Marched from Corinth," page 398, volume 10, "total effective" seems to include "enlisted men for duty," "enlisted men on extra duty" and "enlisted men in arrest" While in Bragg's corps report, part 2, volume 10, page 378, the total effective of Ruggles's division, of Cavalry Brigade, and of seven batteries of artillery is in each case less than the enlisted men present for duty So in the return of First Corps, April 1, 1862, part 2, volume 10, page 382, the total effective and the enlisted men for duty are the same, except as to the infantry of the First Division, where the total effectives is less than the enlisted men present for duty Officers are in no case included in "effective," they are accounted for only in "aggregated "

(n) The cavalry returns are very indefinite Colonel Jordan, page 396, volume 10, gives "total effective cavalry,' 4,382, and this has been assumed to be correct In tabulated statement (ante) Georgia Dragoons, 80, were reported with Third Corps Deduct these and 187 extra-duty men, and we will have 4,115 cavalry present for duty, as shown in recapitulation The cavalry returns of the First, Second, and Third Corps, part 2, volume 10, corresponds with return of cavalry, page 398 volume 10 Neither of these returns include cavalry of Reserve Corps, 785 (see p 877, part 2), nor the unattached cavalry of Wharton and Adams about 1,375

(o) These estimates agree very nearly with Adjutant-General Jordan's report, volume 10, page 396

Effective total (enlisted men only)	40,385
Add proportion of officers, about	3,000
Effective officers and men	43,385
Field returns of April 10, volume 10, page 399	
Effective total, enlisted men, after the battle	52,212
Officers	2,259
Killed, wounded, and missing at Shiloh	10,699
Effective before the battle	45,170
Deduct guard left at Corinth	2,000
	43,170

Still another computation with same result

Total effective enlisted men April 3 (p 398)	....	38,778
Officers	....	2,674
Add cavalry excess, April 10 over April 3 .	.. . .	1,760
Add Hardee's excess, Wood's brigade	....	2,244
		45,451
Deduct Corinth guard ..	.. . .	2,000
		43,451

In Life of Albert Sidney Johnston, by his son, William Preston Johnston, the Confederate forces present at Shiloh are given from tabulated statements on page 398, volume 10, War Records.

No attempt is made to explain the difference between that report and Jordan's report on page 396 or that of Hardee's official report

(p) In his estimate of Grant's "present for duty," April 6, William Preston Johnston enumerates the Fifth Ohio Battery, 137, twice, once with the Second Division and again with the Sixth Division, Munch's Minnesota battery, 126, twice, once with Fifth Division and again with Sixth Division The Fourteenth Wisconsin and Fifteenth Michigan, 1,488, are counted as present on Sunday He omits from his list Carmichael's cavalry, 64, making these corrections, 137+126+1,488−64=1,687, too many by his estimate He gives "present for duty," April 6, five divisions of Grant's army 41,543 Deduct his overestimate of 1,687 leaves 39,856, within 26 of the same number as herein tabulated In William Preston Johnston's estimate of Army of the Ohio he gives its total strength 21,579, making no deduction for troops that did not arrive upon the field until after the battle

(q) The "present for duty," has been taken, in each case, as the number engaged in the battle No attempt has been made to eliminate the noncombatants, because a teamster driving an ammunition wagon or an ambulance is just as necessary as the man with the musket, and just as much a part of the fighting force

If noncombatants were excluded the Union Army would doubtless be reduced to 33,000, the number given by General Grant as "effective present on Sunday" The Confederate Army, by a like computation, would not exceed 40,000, the number claimed by General Johnston

INDEX.

122

O

CPSIA information can be obtained
at www.ICGtesting.com
Printed in the USA
LVHW080530200819
628262LV00012B/216/P

9 780342 975419